HOLISTIC TRAUMA RECOVERY

YOUR PERSONALIZED PATH TO TRANSFORMATION, GROWTH, AND RESILIENCE

SOPHIA L. RAY

Trigger Warning

Trigger warning: This book contains content related to trauma, including descriptions of emotional and psychological distress. Reader discretion is advised for those who may find such topics triggering or distressing. Please prioritize your mental well-being while engaging with this material-holistic healing of trauma.

CONTENTS

INTRODUCTION

Trauma is perhaps the most avoided, ignored, belittled, denied, misunderstood, and untreated cause of human suffering.

— PETER LEVINE

These words, spoken by Peter Levine, resonate deeply with the countless individuals whose lives have been marked by the invisible scars of trauma. Imagine a world where the pain of trauma is not only acknowledged but also holistically understood and addressed. This is the journey we embark upon in the pages of this book—a journey toward holistic trauma recovery.

ANECDOTE ON TRAUMA: A RAY OF LIGHT IN THE DARKNESS

In the quiet corners of Emily's mind, the echoes of a past trauma reverberated, casting shadows over her daily life. For years, she navigated through a world tinged with anxiety and the persistent ache of unresolved pain. The trauma, like an uninvited guest, haunted her steps, coloring her relationships and choices. One day, as Emily sat in a park, lost in thought, she noticed a butterfly fluttering near her. Its delicate wings seemed to carry a message of transformation. Intrigued, she began to observe its graceful dance, unaware that this seemingly ordinary moment would become the turning point.

In that serene setting, as the butterfly gracefully moved from flower to flower, Emily found herself captivated by its resilience and beauty. It was a subtle reminder that even amid the chaos, life had a way of renewing itself. The metamorphosis of the butterfly mirrored the potential for transformation within Emily's own life.

As she watched the butterfly disappear into the horizon, Emily felt a flicker of hope within. The journey of the butterfly became a metaphor for her own path to healing. That day marked the beginning of her exploration into understanding and addressing the trauma that had long held her captive. Little did she know, the seeds of her own metamorphosis had been sown in the quiet beauty of that moment.

Unseen Wounds

In the tapestry of human experience, trauma is an intricate thread often woven silently, leaving behind a narrative of anguish that is both profound and pervasive. To truly grasp the magnitude of this issue, let's delve into a poignant anecdote, a story echoing the sentiments of countless individuals who have wrestled with the aftermath of trauma.

In acknowledging the depth of human suffering caused by trauma, it becomes imperative to recognize the myriad forms this suffering takes. Whether it's the avoidance, denial, belittlement, or misunderstanding of trauma, the pain is real, and it's something many are desperate to escape. If you've picked up this book, it is likely, you are likely intimately acquainted with this pain, seeking a way to navigate through the labyrinth of emotions and experiences that trauma has thrust upon you.

Understanding the catalyst that propels someone to seek out a book on trauma is crucial. It might be the persistent ache of unresolved pain, the haunting memories that refuse to fade, or the realization that conventional approaches to healing have fallen short. Your catalyst might be a moment of clarity, a decision to confront the darkness of the past, or simply the yearning for a better, more fulfilling future.

As you embark on this transformative journey, consider the benefits awaiting you. This guide is your shortcut to understanding, healing, and reclaiming control over your life. You will find practical tools, profound insights, and a holistic approach that transcends conventional methods, offering a comprehensive guide to trauma recovery. In the realm of holistic trauma recovery, success stories abound. From individuals who have rebuilt their lives to celebrities who have openly shared their transformative journeys, the efficacy of the methods outlined in this book is nothing short of extraordinary. Just like anyone else, if you are about to face and conquer your trauma with the principles you are about to discover.

Imagine a life where the shadows of trauma no longer dictate your choices, where everyday life is not a battle but an opportunity for growth. Envision harmonious relationships, a deep sense of self-worth, and the freedom to embrace joy without the looming specter of past pain. This is the result of this guide, my promise to you—a vivid picture of a life unburdened by the chains of trauma is possible.

As you go through the pages of this guide on your journey, the author brings a wealth of expertise and empathy to the table. Their qualifications, experiences, and commitment to holistic trauma recovery make them trustworthy companions on your path to healing. The insights shared in these pages are not just theoretical but from a deep understanding of the complexities of trauma.

Before this holistic approach, the road to trauma recovery was fraught with pitfalls, incomplete solutions, and a lack of understanding of the holistic nature of trauma. The struggle was real; the journey often felt like navigating through a maze with no clear exit. This book represents a paradigm shift, a revelation that transcends traditional methods, providing the missing pieces to complete your personal puzzle of healing.

As you stand at the threshold of this transformative experience, know that this is more than a book; it's a guide to a future free from the weight of trauma. Let the pages ahead be the guide, the solace, and the empowerment you've been seeking. Together, we embark on a path toward healing, understanding, and the profound transformation that awaits you.

1

EXPLORING TRAUMA AND THE PATH TO HEALING

As every therapist will tell you, healing involves discomfort—but so is refusing to heal. And over time, refusing to heal is always more painful.

— RESMAA MENAKEM

In the pages that follow, we embark on a profound journey of self-discovery, growth, and healing. This chapter, the cornerstone of your transformation, is dedicated to exploring the intricate web of trauma that may have shaped your life up until this point. We'll delve into the very essence of trauma, the many forms it can take, and the universal stages of healing that provide the roadmap for your recovery. The key takeaway is understanding the multifaceted nature of trauma and kick-starting your journey toward recovery, while the chapter's goal is to equip you with the knowledge and insights you need to navigate your unique path to healing.

Trauma is a formidable force that often creates changes we don't choose. It's like an invisible hand that shapes our thoughts, emotions, and behaviors. As you read this chapter, you'll come to appreciate that trauma is not a one-size-fits-all concept. It takes on various forms, lurking in the corners of our lives and influencing us in diverse ways. By understanding the nuances of trauma, you'll gain a better perspective on your situation, a critical first step toward recovery.

You see, trauma is not merely about the shockwaves of a catastrophic event or a single moment of crisis. It can be the result of prolonged stress, repeated emotional wounds, or the persistent feeling of being unsafe. It's these subtler forms of trauma that often remain concealed, quietly shaping our lives in profound ways. Yet, just as trauma creates changes we don't choose, healing offers us the power to make changes we do choose. This chapter is your first step in making that choice.

In the following exploration, we'll also journey through the stages of healing. Healing is not a linear path, and it undoubtedly involves discomfort. But remember, as Resmaa Menakem wisely stated, refusing to heal can be even more painful in the long run. By embracing the stages of healing, you'll gain the tools to navigate the discomfort and find solace in the progress you make.

The goal of your journey is clear: To empower you with knowledge and awareness, so you can better understand the impact of trauma on your life and to start your journey toward healing with intention. Whether your trauma is rooted in a specific event or a series of life experiences, the insights shared here will be your guiding light. So, now let's embark on this exploration of trauma, understanding, and healing, knowing that the discomfort we encounter will be the catalyst for positive change.

WHAT IS TRAUMA?

Imagine this: a still, dark lake on a tranquil evening. Its surface, smooth and reflective, conceals the depth beneath. It's much like the concept of trauma-often hidden, its presence betrayed only by the ripples that occasionally break the surface. To embark on our healing journey, we must first grasp the nature of this complex force. So, what is trauma?

According to the American Psychological Association, trauma is defined as the emotional response to a distressing or disturbing event, Psychology Today (Psychology Today Staff, 2023). This response can leave an enduring impact on our mental and emotional well-being. But let's peel back the layers a bit further. Many misconceptions surround the definition of trauma; understanding these misconceptions is vital to our journey. So, let's unravel some of these myths:

- **Trauma is Always Obvious:** One common myth is the belief that trauma is always dramatic and visible, stemming from a major catastrophe or life-threatening situation. However, trauma can take subtler forms. It can emerge from emotional neglect, verbal abuse, or the persistent feeling of being unsafe in one's environment. Trauma is not limited to the stereotypical 'big' events; it can also be born from the 'smaller' ones that erode our sense of security over time.

- **Trauma is the Same for Everyone:** Trauma is highly individual, and its effects can vary from person to person. What's traumatic for one might not be so for another. It depends on various factors, such as personal history, resilience, and support systems. Just because someone else may not understand or validate your experience doesn't mean it's not a valid source of trauma for you.

- **Time Heals All Wounds:** Another common myth is the belief that trauma magically fades with time. While it's true that the intensity of trauma feelings may subside, the effects can linger if left unaddressed. Trauma can create patterns of behavior and thoughts that persist for years, impacting every facet of life.

- **Talking About Trauma Makes it Worse:** Some people avoid discussing their traumatic experiences because they believe it will only make things worse. However, the opposite is often true. Sharing your experiences with a supportive and understanding person or a mental health professional can be a crucial step in the healing process. It allows you to confront the trauma, gain new perspectives, and develop healthy coping strategies.
- **Trauma is Incurable:** Trauma can be incredibly challenging, but it's far from insurmountable. The belief that once trauma has taken root, there's no hope for recovery is a myth. With the right approach and support, you can heal from trauma and build resilience.

Understanding the true nature of trauma and dispelling these misconceptions is a pivotal step in your journey to recovery. Trauma isn't always dramatic, and its effects can linger if ignored. By addressing these misunderstandings and accepting the reality of your experience, you're already on the path to healing.

So, what does all this mean for you, the reader, in your quest for transformation, growth, and resilience? It means that you're not alone in your experience of trauma, and there's hope. It means that you can begin to understand the unique ways trauma has influenced your life and that you have the power to heal.

As we venture deeper into this chapter, we'll explore the various types of trauma, from acute and chronic to complex and developmental. Each type carries its unique characteristics and challenges. By understanding these distinctions, you'll gain a clearer picture of your own experience, making it easier to chart your course toward recovery.

Our journey has only just begun. With the knowledge that trauma isn't confined to stereotypical, dramatic events, you're now better equipped to explore your experience. In the pages to follow, we'll delve deeper into the stages of healing and the practical tools you can employ to emerge from your past stronger and more resilient. Remember, understanding is the first step to healing, and you've already taken that step.

Types of Trauma, Their Symptoms, and Causes

Now that we've demystified the nature of trauma and debunked some common misconceptions let's journey deeper into the intricate world of trauma by exploring its different types, their possible causes, and the symptoms that may arise. By understanding these distinctions, you'll gain a more comprehensive view of your own experiences and how they've shaped your life.

- **Type 1: Acute Trauma:** Acute trauma is the most familiar form of trauma, characterized by a single distressing event that occurs suddenly and often unexpectedly. Car accidents, natural disasters, and assaults are some examples. The symptoms of acute trauma can include flashbacks, nightmares, intense anxiety, and hyperarousal. These symptoms often diminish as time passes but can resurface when triggered by reminders of the traumatic event.

- **Type 2: Chronic Trauma:** Chronic trauma, on the other hand, unfolds over an extended period. It can result from situations where an individual is persistently exposed to distressing or unsafe conditions. Examples include prolonged domestic abuse, ongoing discrimination, or childhood neglect. The symptoms of chronic trauma may consist of pervasive feelings of hopelessness, emotional numbness, and a constant sense of threat. These symptoms can become deeply ingrained and affect daily functioning.

- **Historical, Collective, or Intergenerational Trauma:** Historical, collective, or intergenerational trauma is less about personal experiences and more about the transmission of trauma through generations or a shared community. It often stems from significant historical events, such as genocide, war, or cultural oppression. The symptoms of this type of trauma can manifest as cultural memory, impacting a community's values, beliefs, and behaviors. Healing from intergenerational trauma often involves acknowledging the past and working towards cultural resilience.

- **Vicarious or Secondary Trauma:** Vicarious or secondary trauma is a type that affects you indirectly by experiencing trauma, typically through their professional roles. Healthcare workers, therapists, and first responders may experience vicarious trauma as they bear witness to the suffering of others. Symptoms often mirror those of primary trauma, including nightmares, emotional exhaustion, and a sense of helplessness.
- **Little 't' Trauma:** Little 't' trauma refers to the subtler, everyday events that can be distressing. These events might not be as dramatic as other types of trauma, but they still have a significant impact. Examples include the loss of a pet, a breakup, or workplace bullying. Symptoms can vary widely and may include emotional distress, anxiety, and self-doubt.

SYMPTOMS OF TRAUMA

The symptoms of trauma, regardless of the type, can take a considerable toll on one's mental and emotional well-being. Some of the common symptoms to look out for include:

- **Intrusive Thoughts:** Trauma survivors often experience intrusive thoughts, which are unwelcome, distressing, and persistent memories related to the traumatic event. These thoughts can intrude upon daily life, making it challenging to focus on other tasks. These memories may surface unexpectedly, causing emotional distress and discomfort.

- **Nightmares:** Trauma can lead to recurring nightmares. These nightmares often replay elements of the traumatic event, causing sleep disturbances. You may wake up feeling anxious, fearful, or distressed, further impacting your overall sleep quality and emotional well-being.

- **Hypervigilance**: Hypervigilance is "extreme or excessive vigilance" and "the state of being highly or abnormally alert to potential danger or threat" (Merriam-Webster, n.d.). You may often experience a constant sense of being on edge, with increased irritability, trouble sleeping, and an exaggerated startle response. This constant vigilance can be mentally and emotionally exhausting.

- **Emotional Numbness:** Trauma can lead to emotional numbness or a feeling of being emotionally disconnected. You may find it challenging to experience joy, pleasure, or other positive emotions. This emotional blunting can affect your ability to engage in meaningful and fulfilling activities.

- **Avoidance:** Trauma survivors may engage in avoidance behaviors to cope with reminders of the traumatic event. These reminders could be people, places, or situations that trigger distressing memories. Avoidance often leads to social withdrawal and isolation as you try to shield yourself from potential triggers.

- **Flashbacks:** Flashbacks are vivid and distressing recollections of the trauma. The sights, sounds, and emotions linked to the traumatic flashback may resemble the actual trauma and might feel real in that present moment. These episodes can be profoundly distressing and disorienting.

- **Anxiety:** Trauma often leads to increased anxiety and restlessness. You may find it difficult to relax and may have an overwhelming sense of unease. This constant state of anxiety can impact your daily function and quality of life.

- **Guilt or Self-Blame:** Trauma survivors may grapple with persistent feelings of guilt, self-blame, or shame related to the traumatic event. These feelings can be overwhelming, even when the individual is not responsible for what happened. Self-blame and guilt are common emotional responses to trauma.

- **Difficulty Trusting:** Trauma can erode an individual's ability to trust others. This can manifest as difficulty in forming and maintaining relationships, as survivors may struggle to trust people's intentions or believe that they can be vulnerable without being hurt. Trust issues can impact various aspects of life.

- **Physical Symptoms:** Trauma can manifest physically, with you experiencing symptoms such as headaches, stomachaches, muscle tension, or other physical discomfort. These symptoms often occur without any underlying medical cause and are a manifestation of the psychological and emotional toll of trauma on the body.

These symptoms collectively demonstrate the complex and far-reaching impact of trauma on an individual's mental, emotional, and physical well-being. Addressing these symptoms through therapy, support, and self-care is essential for the healing process.

As you investigate your journey of healing, recognizing these symptoms is crucial. They serve as signposts, helping you to identify the areas in which trauma has left its mark. Remember, the healing process is not a solitary endeavor. Support from professionals, loved ones, and friends can be invaluable on your path to recovery.

Understanding the different types of trauma and their associated symptoms is essential in acknowledging your own experiences. The trauma you've encountered may have characteristics from one or more of these types, and by unraveling the layers, you'll be better equipped to navigate your unique path to healing. In the pages to come, we'll explore the stages of healing and provide you with practical tools to begin your transformation journey. With every page turned, you're moving closer to a life marked by resilience, growth, and a newfound sense of peace!

NEUROBIOLOGY OF TRAUMA

The neurobiology of trauma is a complex and fascinating subject, shedding light on how our brains are fundamentally altered by the distressing experiences we endure. To truly understand the nature of trauma and its consequences, we must venture into the realm of neuroscience. Recent research and case studies by Neuroscience News (*How Trauma Changes the Brain*, 2022) provide invaluable insights into the neurobiology of trauma. By examining the brain's responses to traumatic events, we gain a deeper appreciation of the lasting changes that can occur. Let's delve into the fascinating world of how trauma shapes the brain:

Salience Network: The Brain's Alarm System

One crucial aspect of the neurobiology of trauma revolves around the brain's "salience network." This network acts as our alarm system, detecting and responding to stimuli in our environment. When confronted with trauma, this system goes into overdrive, hyperfocusing on the distressing event. Studies have shown that you have experienced trauma and exhibit heightened activity in the salience network. It's as if the brain becomes hypersensitive to potential threats.

Research conducted by the University of Rochester Medical Center (Suarez-Jimenez, 2022) reveals that this heightened salience network activity can persist long after the traumatic event. This persistent hyperactivity can lead to symptoms such as hypervigilance, where the individual remains in a constant state of alertness, and intrusive thoughts that replay elements of the trauma.

CHANGING BRAIN STRUCTURES: THE AMYGDALA AND HIPPOCAMPUS

The amygdala and hippocampus are two brain structures profoundly affected by trauma. The amygdala, often referred to as the brain's emotional center, plays a significant role in processing emotions, particularly those related to fear and anxiety. Research done by Amy Marschall, PsyD (Marschall, 2023) shows that the amygdala can become overactive if you with a history of trauma. This heightened activity can result in increased emotional reactivity and difficulty regulating emotions.

In contrast, the hippocampus, responsible for forming new memories and regulating stress responses, can experience a decrease in volume and function in response to trauma. This can lead to difficulties in memory consolidation and an impaired ability to manage stress. Imagine your brain as a complex network of connections, each influenced by the traumatic event you've experienced. These structural changes can explain why trauma survivors often have vivid, distressing memories and struggle with emotional regulation.

Complex Interaction: The Prefrontal Cortex

The prefrontal cortex, responsible for decision-making, impulse control, and complex thinking, plays a crucial role in managing our reactions to stress and emotions. If you have experienced trauma, the prefrontal cortex may become less active. This can result in difficulties in regulating emotions and impulsivity. In essence, it's as if the brain's rational, calming center is temporarily disabled.

To further illustrate the profound effects of trauma on the brain, Let's consider a real-life case study. Sarah, a survivor of a car accident, had vivid flashbacks of the traumatic event that left her emotionally distressed. Neuroimaging studies revealed increased activity in her amygdala, highlighting her heightened emotional reactivity. Her prefrontal cortex, responsible for modulating emotions and regulating stress responses, showed decreased activity.

What this case study demonstrates is that the neurobiological impact of trauma is not a hypothetical construct but a real, observable phenomenon. Understanding how trauma influences the brain can help trauma survivors like Sarah make sense of their symptoms and why they experience intrusive thoughts, heightened emotional responses, and difficulties in decision-making and impulse control. The neurobiology of trauma is a captivating field of study, unveiling the intricate ways trauma shapes our brains. By comprehending these changes, you're better equipped to navigate the path to healing.

SIGNS YOU'RE SUPPRESSING TRAUMA

We've looked into the nature of trauma, its many forms, and how it shapes the human brain. But what happens when we suppress trauma, hiding it deep within ourselves? Repression versus suppression, the signs of suppressed trauma in adults, and how trauma can impact our lives are all facets we must understand as we navigate the path to healing.

Repression versus Suppression

Repression and suppression are two psychological defense mechanisms we employ when faced with painful memories or experiences. Understanding the distinction between them is essential to grasp how we can unintentionally hide trauma from ourselves.

Repression is like the subconscious act; wherein distressing memories are blocked from conscious awareness. It's as if the mind tucks these memories away in a hidden, locked room. Repression often occurs as a protective mechanism to shield us from overwhelming emotional pain.

Suppression, on the other hand, is a conscious effort to push distressing memories aside. It's as if we acknowledge the memories but keep them out of our immediate thoughts. Suppression can be a temporary coping strategy, but if it becomes chronic, it may lead to the long-term suppression of trauma.

So, what are the signs of suppressed trauma in adults? They often manifest in various ways:

- **Unexplained Anxiety and Fear**: You may experience high levels of anxiety and irritation fear without a clear trigger. These emotions are often linked to suppressed traumatic memories affecting your emotional state.
- **Uncontrollable Mood Swings:** Rapid and intense mood swings, from anger and irritability to sadness and despair, can be indicative of unresolved trauma. These emotions are simmering beneath the surface, seeking expression.
- **Chronic Health Issues:** Suppressed trauma can take a toll on your physical health. It's common to experience unexplained aches, pains, and even autoimmune conditions as the body reacts to internalized stress.
- **Nightmares and Flashbacks:** Even though you may not consciously remember the traumatic event, it can haunt your dreams and invade your waking moments through flashbacks.
- **Emotional Numbness:** You could have suppressed trauma and may become emotionally numb. It's as if you've locked away your feelings to avoid confronting the painful memories.
- **Relationship Struggles:** Suppressed trauma can affect your ability to form and maintain healthy

relationships. You may struggle with trust, intimacy, or emotional connection.

- **Self-Destructive Behavior:** Coping with suppressed trauma can lead to self-destructive behavior such as substance abuse, self-harm, or reckless actions. These behaviors serve as unhealthy outlets for the pain you're suppressing.

As we've explored the signs of suppressed trauma, it's important to understand how trauma can infiltrate various aspects of our lives. The impact of trauma is far-reaching, touching not only our mental health but also our physical well-being, relationships, and more.

How Trauma Can Affect Your Life

Trauma can significantly affect your mental health, leading to conditions such as depression, anxiety, post-traumatic stress disorder (PTSD), and even dissociation. Symptoms can include intrusive thoughts, flashbacks, and overwhelming emotional responses. It's important to acknowledge and address these challenges to promote mental well-being.

The physical toll of suppressed trauma can be immense. Chronic stress related to trauma can weaken the immune system, increase the risk of chronic health conditions, and lead to unhealthy coping mechanisms such as substance abuse. It's essential to prioritize self-care and seek support to maintain your overall health.

Suppressed trauma can interfere with your ability to form healthy connections with others. Trust issues, emotional distancing, and difficulty with vulnerability are common challenges. Addressing your trauma can help you build stronger, more fulfilling relationships.

Trauma can disrupt daily life in many ways. It can lead to difficulty concentrating, poor impulse control, and a reduced ability to cope with stress. Seeking professional help and employing healthy coping strategies can mitigate these challenges.

The neurobiology of trauma, the sign of suppressed trauma, and the impact trauma has on our lives are interconnected and complex. Recognizing the signs and seeking help is a courageous step toward healing. This journey is about understanding, healing, and ultimately reclaiming your life from the shadows of trauma. You are not alone on this path, and hope and support are available to help you emerge from the shadows of your past into the light of a healthier future.

The Road to Recovery

First and foremost, I want to assure you that recovery from trauma is not just possible; it's a significant achievement. You may have been struggling with a range of symptoms and emotional distress, but with the right support and resources, you can regain control over your life and well-being.

- **Acknowledging the Problem and Seeking Help:** Understand that acknowledging the impact of trauma on your life and recognizing the need for support can be a daunting but crucial first step. It takes great strength to seek help, whether through therapy, support groups, or self-help resources. This self-awareness opens the door to healing.
- **Partial Recovery Matters:** It's important to remember that trauma recovery is not an all-or-nothing process. Even partial recovery can make a significant difference in your life. Healing is not always a linear journey; there may be ups and downs along the way. It is important to celebrate the small victories on the recovery journey, as any progress you make improves your overall well-being.
- **Building Resilience:** Throughout the recovery process, you have the opportunity to build resilience and coping strategies. These not only help you overcome the impact of trauma but also prepare you to face challenges with greater strength. Recovery is an opportunity for personal growth and increased self-awareness.

PHASES/STAGES OF TRAUMA RECOVERY

Recovery from trauma often involves various phases or stages, which may vary in duration and intensity for each person. You may revisit certain stages as you continue your healing journey. Here are common phases of trauma recovery.

- **Safety and Stabilization:** This initial phase focuses on creating a sense of safety and stability. This may involve developing coping strategies, establishing routines, and seeking support from a therapist or support group.
- **Remembering and Mourning:** In this phase, you begin to remember and process the traumatic events. You confront painful memories and emotions, which can be distressing but are essential for healing.
- **Reconnection:** Reconnection involves rebuilding relationships, reconnecting with yourself, and learning to trust others. It often requires addressing trust issues and working on interpersonal skills.
- **Integration:** Integration is the stage where you integrate your traumatic experiences into your personal narratives and life stories. It is about making sense of what happened and how it has shaped you.
- **Moving forward:** The final phase involves moving forward with life, setting goals, and re-engaging with a sense of purpose and meaning. It is about finding hope and envisioning a brighter future.

THING TO REMEMBER

As you embark on your journey to recovery, there are some important things to keep in mind:

- **Patience:** Recovery takes time, so be patient with yourself. Avoid rushing the process or expecting instant results. Healing is a gradual journey.
- **Self-Care:** Prioritize self-care practices that nurture your physical, emotional, and mental well-being. This may include exercise, relaxation techniques, and engaging in enjoyable activities.
- **Seeking Professional Help:** Consider working with a mental health professional specializing in trauma. You can find guidance and support according to your specific needs from therapy.
- **Support System:** Your friends and family who understand your journey can provide much-needed emotional support while you embark on your healing journey.
- **Avoid Self-Criticism:** Be gentle with yourself and avoid self-criticism. Healing is not a linear process, and setbacks are normal. Treat yourself with compassion.
- **Holistic Approach:** A holistic approach to recovery, including a combination of therapies, self-help resources, and self-discovery, can be highly effective. It addresses your whole being, body, and spirit.

Recovery from trauma is not only possible but also a trans-formative journey. Acknowledging the problem, seeking help, and recognizing the value of even partial recovery are crucial steps in your path to healing and personal renewal. Understanding the phases of trauma recovery and remembering key principles like patience, self-care, and the importance of a support system can guide you on your journey. While the road may be challenging, it leads to regaining control, resilience, and a brighter future.

As we conclude this chapter, it's clear that trauma's profound impact reaches every corner of our lives, from our mental and physical well-being to our relationships and daily existence. The road to recovery may be challenging, but it is possible, marked by hope, resilience, and transformative healing. Building on these insights, the next chapter will delve into strengthening emotional resilience, equipping you with the tools to adapt to the trauma you've endured.

2

THE ART OF BOUNCING BACK— NURTURING EMOTIONAL RESILIENCE AGAINST TRAUMA

Wounds won't heal the way you want them to; they heal the way they need to.

— DELE OLANUBI

In the aftermath of trauma, when the wounds run deep and the path to healing seems uncertain, we find ourselves in pursuit of a profound quality: emotional resilience. This is where we aim to equip you with the power to adapt and overcome the trauma you've encountered. It is a journey that begins with an understanding of resilience's vital role in the process of recovery.

The healing process is personal, unique, and often guided by the strength of emotional resilience. In the following pages, we will explore what emotional resilience is, its types, its associated traits, and most importantly, why nurturing emotional resilience matters on your path to trauma recovery. With each insight gained, you'll be better equipped to navigate the challenges ahead, embrace your own unique healing journey, and ultimately transform your trauma into a source of strength.

THE IMPORTANCE OF EMOTIONAL RESILIENCE

Emotional resilience is the invisible armor that empowers you to not only endure the most challenging of life's trials but to emerge from them stronger, wiser, and more prepared for the future. It is the ability to adapt, bounce back from adversity, and retain one's psychological and emotional well-being in the face of turmoil. In the context of trauma recovery, emotional resilience plays a pivotal role, offering a guiding light through the darkness of past experiences and the journey toward healing.

Understanding Resilience

Resilience is the capacity to recover from life's setbacks and adapt positively to adversity. The inner strength enables you to navigate hardships without being overwhelmed by them. While some might view resilience as an innate quality, research suggests that it can be developed and nurtured, providing hope for those on the path to trauma recovery. There are several types of resilience, each offering unique strengths and coping mechanisms:

- **Emotional Resilience:** This type focuses on managing emotions effectively, especially during distressing situations. Emotional resilience involves self-awareness, empathy, and the ability to express one's feelings constructively.
- **Mental Resilience:** Mental resilience involves cognitive flexibility, problem-solving skills, and adaptability. It's the ability to find solutions and perspective amid adversity.
- **Social Resilience:** This resilience type centers on maintaining and nurturing healthy relationships. It involves effective communication, empathy, and the ability to seek and offer support.
- **Physical Resilience:** Physical resilience relates to maintaining good health and well-being, both mentally and physically. It includes practices like exercise, nutrition, and stress management.
- **Spiritual Resilience:** Spiritual resilience encompasses one's core beliefs and values. It provides a sense of purpose and meaning in life, helping you find strength in your faith or personal philosophy.

The Traits of Resilience

The building blocks of life are the traits of resilience. Several key traits underpin emotional resilience, making it a crucial asset in trauma recovery.

- **Self-Awareness.** Recognizing one's own emotions and reactions is a fundamental aspect of resilience. It enables you to process your feelings and make conscious choices in response to adversity.
- **Adaptability.** Emotional resilience is closely linked to adaptability, the ability to adjust to changing circumstances. It allows you to find new ways to tackle challenges and navigate unexpected hurdles.
- **Empathy.** Being able to understand and share the feelings of others fosters positive social connections, a cornerstone of resilience. In trauma recovery, empathy can build a support network and offer comfort.
- **Problem-Solving Skills.** Resilient individuals are adept problem solvers. They approach difficulties as opportunities for growth, applying creative and effective solutions to complex challenges.
- **Emotional Regulation.** Emotional resilience entails the capacity to manage intense emotions without being overwhelmed by them. This trait aids in maintaining composure during distressing moments.
- **Optimism.** A positive outlook and hope for the future are pivotal aspects of resilience. Optimism

fuels the belief that challenges can be overcome and that there is light at the end of the tunnel.

The Significance of Emotional Resilience in Trauma Recovery

Now, let's explore why emotional resilience is of paramount importance in trauma recovery. When we face traumatic experiences, our emotional well-being is often shaken to the core. Emotional resilience is the lifeline that helps us navigate these stormy seas.

- **Coping with Triggers**. Trauma survivors often face triggers that can revive painful memories. Emotional resilience equips us with the tools to cope with these triggers, manage intense emotions, and prevent overwhelming distress.
- **Positive Adaption.** Resilience allows survivors to adapt positively to the changes brought about by trauma. It empowers them to find new perspectives, solutions, and a sense of meaning in their experiences.
- **Maintaining Mental Health.** Traumatic experiences can lead to mental health challenges such as anxiety and depression. Emotional resilience supports mental well-being by fostering a positive outlook and helping us manage our emotional responses.
- **Forming Health Relationships.** Emotional resilience facilitates the formation and maintenance of healthy relationships. It involves empathy,

communication, and the ability to seek and offer support, all crucial for building a reliable support network.

- **Preventing Relapse.** Emotional resilience plays a significant role in preventing the relapse of trauma-related symptoms. It empowers survivors to manage distressing emotions and maintain emotional well-being over time.
- **Reclaiming control.** Trauma often leaves you feeling helpless. Emotional resilience helps survivors regain a sense of control over their lives, providing a foundation for recovery and personal growth.

Emotional resilience is the cornerstone of trauma recovery. It provides the emotional and psychological strength needed to navigate the complex terrain of healing, adapt to adversity, and emerge from trauma with newfound strength and wisdom. As you venture further into this chapter, you will discover practical ways to nurture and strengthen your emotional resilience to equip yourself to face your trauma with courage, hope, and resilience.

MINDSET

The journey to trauma recovery is an intricate one, and at its core lies the potent influence of mindset. A healthy mindset serves as a sturdy bridge between the past and the future, helping us navigate the challenges of trauma recovery with courage, hope, and resilience. Mindset plays a profound role in our ability to heal, grow, and thrive in the aftermath of trauma. Cultivating a healthy mindset for trauma recovery is like tending to the garden of your soul. It requires careful nurturing and mindful practices. The impact of a healthy mindset is evident in various key aspects, each contributing to your journey of healing and transformation.

Being Positive to Overcome Shadows

The aftermath of trauma often leaves us grappling with negative thought patterns and cognitive distortions. These persistent shadows can cast a long, dark cloud over the path to recovery. However, staying positive after trauma is not only possible but also essential for healing. Here are some insights into how to maintain positivity after trauma:

- **Challenge Cognitive Distortions:** Cognitive distortions are habitual ways of thinking not based on reality. They include all-or-nothing thinking, catastrophizing, and personalization. Identifying and challenging these distortions is a crucial step towards positivity.
- **Practice Self-Compassion:** Treating yourself with the same kindness and understanding you would offer to a dear friend can be transformative. Self-compassion fosters positivity and helps counteract self-criticism.

- **Cultivate Gratitude:** Practicing gratitude can shift your focus from what you've lost to what you still have. Regularly reflecting on what you're thankful for can boost your overall outlook.
- **Surround Yourself with Positivity:** Seek out sources of positivity, whether through supportive relationships, inspiring content, or engaging in activities that bring you joy.

Being Solution-Focused

A crucial facet of a healthy mindset in trauma recovery is being solution-focused rather than problem-focused. Problem-focused thinking fixates on the challenges and obstacles, while solution-focused thinking seeks answers and opportunities. Here's how to be more of the latter:

- **Identify the issue.** Begin by recognizing the problem or challenge you're facing. Clearly defining the issue is the first step in finding a solution.
- **Brainstorm solutions.** Once you've identified the problem, brainstorm possible solutions. Encourage creativity, and don't limit yourself to conventional approaches.
- **Take small steps.** Break down the solution into manageable steps. This makes the process less overwhelming and allows for steady progress.
- **Seek support.** Don't hesitate to seek help or guidance from others. Sometimes, a fresh

perspective can provide insights you might have missed.

Looking at the Bigger picture

Big-picture thinking, or psychological decentering, is a practice that helps you broaden your perspective. It encourages you to see beyond the immediate challenges and adopt a more holistic view. Here's why it's beneficial for your mental well-being:

- Psychological decentering can alleviate stress by diminishing the perceived magnitude of immediate issues. It reminds you that life is a continuum, and today's problems are just part of a larger tapestry.
- Big-picture thinking instills resilience by teaching you to view challenges as opportunities for growth. It encourages you to find meaning and purpose in your experiences.
- A broader perspective aids in better decision-making. It allows you to consider long-term consequences and weigh options more effectively.

Strategies and exercises can help you learn to "zoom out" and adopt a big-picture mindset. Try exercises like mindfulness, journaling, or engaging in activities that connect you with nature. These practices can gradually shift your focus from the minutiae to the grandeur of life.

Learning From Your Mistakes

Transitioning from a phase of learning from your mistakes to embracing a growth mindset is a pivotal moment in trauma recovery. Initially, the focus is often on analyzing and understanding past missteps and how they relate to your traumatic experiences. However, the shift towards a growth mindset signifies the profound realization that these very mistakes are not indicators of weakness but growth opportunities. It's about recognizing that healing is not a linear path and setbacks are part of the journey. By viewing these challenges as stepping stones toward personal development and resilience, you empower yourself to approach your recovery with optimism, adaptability, and a profound belief in your potential to transform and heal.

WHAT IS A GROWTH MINDSET?

A growth mindset is a term coined by psychologist Carol Dweck (Dweck, 2015). It refers to the belief that your abilities, intelligence, and qualities can be developed and improved over time through dedication and hard work, while a fixed mindset is the belief that your abilities are inherent and permanent. In other words, a growth mindset is about seeing challenges and setbacks as opportunities for learning and growth, while a fixed mindset tends to view these challenges as threats to one's self-esteem.

The Power of a Growth Mindset in Trauma Recovery

Understanding the significance of a growth mindset in the context of trauma recovery is essential:

- **Embracing Resilience and Grit:** Trauma recovery is undoubtedly a challenging journey. A growth mindset can help you embrace the difficulties and setbacks as part of the process rather than as insurmountable obstacles. It encourages you to view these challenges as opportunities to develop resilience and grit.

- **Reframing Mistakes as Learning:** A growth mindset encourages you to reframe mistakes as valuable learning experiences. In trauma recovery, this means recognizing that setbacks, triggers, and difficult emotions are not signs of failure but natural parts of the healing process. It empowers you to analyze what went wrong, adapt your strategies, and continue growing.

- **Openness to Change:** Trauma can lead to rigid thought patterns and a fear of change. A growth mindset fosters adaptability and openness to change, which are essential for healing. It helps you explore new coping strategies and therapies, embrace new perspectives, and evolve as a person.

CULTIVATING A GROWTH MINDSET

Developing a growth mindset is a transformative process that takes time and commitment. Here are some tips to help you cultivate a growth mindset during your trauma recovery:

- Start by recognizing whether you have a fixed or growth mindset. Self-awareness is the first step toward change. Be honest with yourself about your beliefs regarding your ability to recover from trauma.
- If you discover that you have a fixed mindset, challenge those beliefs. Remind yourself that you have the capacity to change and grow. Your past does not dictate your entire future.
- Instead of avoiding challenges, welcome them. Embrace the discomfort and difficulties as opportunities for personal growth. These challenges are not signs of your inadequacy but stepping stones toward recovery.
- When you encounter setbacks or triggers in your recovery journey, don't view them as failures. Instead, analyze what led to these setbacks and consider how you can adapt your approach. What can you learn from this experience?
- Set specific, achievable goals for your recovery. As you make progress, celebrate your accomplishments,

no matter how small they may seem. Recognizing your growth reinforces the idea that you are on the right path.

- Connect with therapists, support groups, or individuals who can encourage your growth mindset. Surrounding yourself with people who believe in your potential can be highly motivating. Surround yourself with a support network that encourages your growth mindset. Share your progress, setbacks, and insights with those who uplift and inspire you.

- Foster a positive outlook on your recovery journey. Replace self-criticism with self-compassion. Remember that healing is a process, and each step forward, no matter how small, is a step toward resilience.

- Regularly reflect on your thoughts and attitudes. Are they fostering a growth mindset or holding you back? Self-reflection is a powerful tool for self-improvement.

- Understand that healing from trauma is a process that takes time. Embrace the journey with an open mind and be patient with yourself.

- Keep a journal to record your progress and insights. Document how you've overcome challenges and what you've learned from your experiences.

- Challenge negative self-talk and replace it with

affirmations that reflect your belief in your capacity
to recover.

- Educate yourself about the principles of a growth
mindset. Read books, attend workshops, and engage
in activities that promote personal growth and
resilience.

A growth mindset is a powerful mindset to adopt in trauma
recovery. It enables you to embrace challenges, view
setbacks as opportunities for learning, and cultivate
resilience and grit. By acknowledging your current mindset,
challenging negative beliefs, and consistently embracing the
principles of growth, you can navigate the recovery journey
with renewed hope and determination.

Being Patient with Yourself

Patience is a powerful ally of trauma recovery. It's crucial to
remember that healing is a process, and progress may not
always be linear. Being patient with yourself means allowing
the time and space needed for your growth and recovery.
Here are some tips to cultivate this patience:

- **Practice Self-Compassion.** In your pursuit of
healing, extend to yourself the same kindness and
understanding you would offer to a dear friend. It's
essential to acknowledge that healing isn't a race; it's
a deeply personal journey that deserves the time and
care it demands.

- **Set Realistic Expectations.** Define your recovery goals and timelines with realism and gentleness. The healing process should not be trusted or pressured; it requires the freedom to evolve at its own pace. Setting realistic expectations empowers you to respect your journey.
- **Seek Support.** You need not navigate the path to recovery alone. Reach out to friends, family, or professionals who can provide the guidance, encouragement, and solace you may require. Support can be a significant source of comfort and strength.
- **Celebrate Small Wins.** Every step forward in your recovery, regardless of how minor it may seem, is a triumph worthy of acknowledgment and celebration. These small victories accumulate, fostering a sense of progress and hope as you continue on your journey toward healing.

The power of a mindset in trauma recovery cannot be overstated. Cultivating a healthy mindset involves embracing positivity, solution-focused thinking, big-picture perspectives, and a growth mindset. It also requires the patience to understand that healing is a journey, not a destination. By incorporating these principles into your life, you can build a resilient mindset that will not only guide you through trauma recovery but also lead you toward a future of hope, strength, and transformation.

Common Trauma-Related Reactions

In the wake of a traumatic event, we often grapple with a complex array of emotional and psychological reactions. These responses are a natural part of the human experience when confronted with trauma, as the mind and body strive to cope, adapt, and heal. Understanding these common trauma-related reactions is crucial not only for those directly affected but also for the support systems surrounding them. There are various ways people react to trauma, as we all uniquely experience trauma.

- **Flashbacks and Intrusive Memories.** One of the most frequently encountered trauma-related reactions is the intrusion of distressing memories into daily life. These intrusions can take the form of flashbacks, vivid and distressing recollections of the traumatic event, or intrusive thoughts that emerge unexpectedly. For example, consider a combat veteran who may experience vivid flashbacks of the battlefield when exposed to loud noises or certain scents, even when no immediate threat is present.

- **Avoidance and Numbing.** In an attempt to shield ourselves from the overwhelming emotions associated with trauma, many of us may resort to avoidance behaviors. This might include steering clear of places, people, or situations reminiscent of the traumatic event. For example, a survivor of a severe car accident may avoid driving or even riding in a car altogether due to the intense fear and anxiety triggered by the memories of the crash.

- **Hypervigilance and Startle Responses.** Trauma can lead to heightened vigilance and an exaggerated startle response. We become hyper-attuned to potential threats in our environments, leading to heightened anxiety and constant alertness. A survivor of a home invasion. For instance, might become hyper-vigilant, installing multiple security systems and experiencing severe jumps from slightly unexpected noise.

- **Emotional Numbness.** It is not uncommon for trauma survivors to experience emotional numbing. In this reaction, you find it challenging to connect with or express your emotions. You may feel emotionally detached, as if you're merely going through the motions of life. An example might be a sexual assault survivor who feels emotionally disconnected from their own body and struggles to connect with their desires and feelings.

- **Sleep Disturbances.** Trauma can significantly disrupt one's sleep patterns, leading to insomnia, nightmares, or night sweats. Sleep disturbances often exacerbate other trauma-related reactions, as a lack of restful sleep can make it challenging to manage emotions and cognitive functions. A real-life example is a military veteran who experiences frequent nightmares of combat, leading to sleep deprivation and increased daytime anxiety.

- **Irritability and Anger.** Trauma can manifest as increased irritability and anger, often stemming from a sense of powerlessness and frustration. The traumatic event may have left you feeling helpless or violated, fueling these intense emotions. An example might be a child who experienced bullying at school and now exhibits irritability and outbursts of anger when confronted with social situations.
- **Changes in Beliefs and Worldview.** Trauma can shatter our previously held beliefs and worldviews. This transformation can be profound, leading to existential questions and a reevaluation of life's purpose and meaning. For instance, a survivor of a life-threatening illness may undergo a profound change in their beliefs and priorities, leading to a redefined sense of purpose.
- **Social Withdrawal.** Many trauma survivors experience social withdrawal, which can result from feelings of shame, guilt, or fear of judgment. Someone who has faced the trauma of divorce may become socially withdrawn, avoiding friends and family gatherings due to the perceived stigma associated with marital dissolution.
- **Physical Symptoms.** Trauma-related reactions can also manifest as physical symptoms. Chronic headaches, gastrointestinal issues, and increased

susceptibility to illness are not uncommon. These physical symptoms often occur alongside emotional and psychological responses to trauma, compounding the individual's distress. For instance, a victim of domestic violence may experience chronic migraines and gastrointestinal problems as a result of prolonged stress and fear.

- **Substance Abuse and Self-Harming Behaviors.** Unfortunately, some individuals turn to substance abuse or self-harming behaviors as a way to cope with the emotional pain stemming from trauma. This reaction can lead to a dangerous cycle of addiction and self-destructive tendencies. An individual who experienced childhood abuse might turn to substance abuse as a way to numb their emotional pain.

- **Re-Experiencing Triggers.** Think about encountering triggers that transport you back to the traumatic moment. It's like being thrown into a turbulent storm of anxiety and panic. These triggers can be sights, sounds, or situations that resemble the traumatic event, unleashing a cascade of distressing memories.

Understanding these common trauma-related reactions is the first step in your healing journey. By recognizing and addressing these responses, you can begin to regain control over your life, reclaim your strength, and find your path to resilience and transformation. Remember, you are not alone, and support and healing are awaiting you.

Emotional Regulation and Self-Control

Emotional regulation refers to the ability to manage and modulate one's emotions effectively while focusing on positivity and a sense of calm, according to Psychology Today Staff (2019). It involves the conscious and subconscious processes that enable you to respond to your feelings in adaptive ways. In essence, it's about maintaining emotional equilibrium and preventing extremes of emotion from taking control over your emotions and reactions in the present moment, enabling you to notice your emotions and taking an active step to remain calm and focused without anxiety or anger driving your reactions.

HEALTHY EMOTIONAL REGULATION STRATEGIES

- **Mindfulness and Meditation:** Practicing mindfulness techniques or meditation can help you become more aware of your emotions and develop a greater capacity to stay present in the moment.
- **Deep Breathing Exercises**: Engaging in deep breathing exercises, such as diaphragmatic breathing, can help reduce stress and anxiety, promoting emotional balance.
- **Physical Activity:** Regular physical exercise releases

endorphins, which are natural mood boosters and stress relievers.

- **Social Support:** Seeking support from friends, family, or therapists can provide an outlet for emotional expression and understanding.
- **Journaling:** Keeping a journal to express thoughts and emotions can be a therapeutic way to process and regulate feelings.
- **Cognitive Behavior Techniques**: Cognitive behavioral therapy (CBT) helps you to identify negative thoughts, beliefs, and behaviors and challenge these patterns to enable you to decrease their contribution to your emotional distress (*Cognitive Behavioral Therapy (CBT)*, 2018).
- **Self-Care Practices:** Engaging in self-care activities like taking a bath, practicing hobbies, or spending quality time alone can help restore emotional balance.

UNHEALTHY EMOTIONAL REGULATION STRATEGIES

- **Avoidance**: Avoiding emotional triggers or distressing situations may provide temporary relief but does not address the underlying issues.
- **Suppression**: Suppressing emotions by bottling them up can lead to emotional outbursts or prolonged distress later on.

- **Substance Abuse**: Turning to drugs or alcohol as a coping mechanism can lead to addiction and worsen emotional problems.
- **Self-Harm**: Engaging in self-harming behaviors, such as cutting, is a dangerous way to cope with emotional pain.
- **Isolation:** Withdrawing from social interactions can exacerbate feelings of loneliness and depression.
- **Escapism:** Using distractions like excessive television, video games, or social media to escape emotions can prevent emotional processing.
- **Emotional Eating**: Overeating or binge eating to cope with emotional distress may lead to health problems and worsen emotional regulation.

It's an election to recognize the difference between healthy and unhealthy emotional regulation strategies to develop effective coping mechanisms and promote emotional well-being during the trauma recovery process.

WHAT IS EMOTIONAL DYSREGULATION

Emotional dysregulation, as explained by Cleveland Clinic (*Emotional Dysregulation*, n.d.), is a condition where an individual finds it hard to manage or control their emotions and reactions to their feelings effectively, often leading to outbursts of anger or extreme mood swings. It can manifest as intense emotional reactions, mood swings, and difficulty returning to a state of emotional equilibrium after experiencing strong feelings. Dysregulation can impair one's ability to function in daily life, maintain relationships, and make rational decisions.

EMOTIONAL CYCLE AND HOW TO BREAK IT

The emotional cycle is a pattern of emotional dysregulation where intense emotions trigger impulsive or unhelpful behaviors, leading to negative consequences, which, in turn, intensify the emotions. This cycle can be challenging to break, but it is crucial for achieving emotional regulation. Here's the step-by-step process:

- **Recognize Triggers.** The first step is to identify the emotional triggers. These are situations, thoughts, or external stimuli that initiate intense emotional responses. Trauma triggers, in particular, can be deeply ingrained and may require professional guidance for identification.

- **Pause and Reflect**. When you feel triggered, take a moment to pause and reflect. This is the crucial moment when you can choose how to respond. Mindfulness techniques, such as deep breathing, can help you stay in the present and prevent impulsive reactions.
- **Emotional Labeling.** Labeling your emotions helps create a mental distance between you and your feelings, making it easier to regulate them.
- **Emotional Regulation Strategies.** Implement healthy emotional regulation strategies, such as cognitive reappraisal, self-soothing, and trigger identification (which we will explore in detail below). These strategies can help you regain control over your emotions and respond more adaptively.

EMOTIONAL REGULATION STRATEGIES

Emotional regulation strategies are powerful tools for achieving emotional balance. Let's explore three key strategies that can facilitate emotional regulation:

Cognitive Reappraisal: Cognitive reappraisal is a potent strategy that empowers you to reshape your emotional responses by altering your interpretation of a situation. It involves a fundamental shift in perspective, allowing you to mitigate these emotional reactions and foster a more balanced outlook.

Sample Practice: Imagine you've received constructive criticism at work, and your initial emotional response is frustration. Instead of dwelling on the criticism and letting it escalate your emotional state, you can practice cognitive reappraisal. Challenge your initial thought by asking yourself questions like, "Is this feedback an opportunity for growth?" or " Is my emotional reaction proportional to the situation?" By considering alternative, more balanced interpretations, you can diminish the intensity of your emotional response and respond more rationally.

Cognitive reappraisal is a skill that can be honed through practice and self-awareness. Over time, it can significantly enhance your emotional regulation by providing a means to reframe thoughts and emotions more healthily.

Self-Soothing: Self-soothing techniques are invaluable for calming emotional distress at the moment. They are centered on the idea of providing emotional comfort to oneself and creating a sense of safety and security. These techniques are particularly effective for managing acute emotional responses and reducing their intensity.

Sample Case Study: Consider a scenario where you find yourself overwhelmed by anxiety during a stressful work presentation. In this situation, self-soothing can be a highly practical strategy. You might employ deep breathing exercises to regain a sense of calm, focus on positive self-talk to counteract negative thoughts or use physical methods like gently rubbing your fingers together to ground yourself in the present moment. Applying these self-soothing techniques allows you to navigate the challenging situation with a more collected and emotionally balanced demeanor.

Self-soothing strategies, as mentioned above, vary from person to person and can be adjusted to your unique needs and comfort. The goal is to provide emotional comfort and alleviate distress, ultimately fostering emotional regulation.

Trigger Identification: Trauma triggers are powerful catalysts for emotional dysregulation. Identifying these triggers is essential for effective emotional regulation and is often a complex and nuanced process. Trauma triggers can be external stimuli, thoughts, or situations that activate intense emotional responses, often linked to past traumatic experiences.

Understanding Trauma Triggers: Trauma triggers can vary widely between individuals. They may be associated with specific sounds, sights, smells, or even emotional states. Identifying trauma triggers is a personal and introspective journey. It often involves working with a mental health professional who can guide you through the process. The process may include journaling, discussions, and self-reflection to pinpoint patterns and recognize the unique triggers that cause emotional dysregulation.

> **Sample Coping Strategies:** Coping with trauma triggers is a multifaceted endeavor, and it often requires a tailored approach. Some strategies for managing trauma triggers include exposure therapy, grounding techniques, and professional therapeutic interventions.

Emotional regulation is an ongoing journey that may involve the integration of several strategies. By practicing cognitive reappraisal, self-soothing techniques, and effectively managing trauma triggers, you can achieve greater control over your emotional responses. These strategies empower you to lead a more balanced and fulfilling life by addressing emotional dysregulation and fostering emotional well-being. Remember that emotional regulation is a skill that can be honed over time. As you explore these strategies, you'll find yourself better equipped to navigate the intricate realm of your emotions.

Resilience-Building Exercises

Resilience is the ability to bounce back from adversity, navigate life's challenges with courage, and grow stronger through difficult times. It's a skill that's especially valuable in today's fast-paced and unpredictable world. Here are ten resilience-building exercises that are designed to empower you to foster greater mental strength and emotional resilience.

Resilience-building exercises contribute to emotional regulation and enhance your overall emotional awareness. By cultivating resilience, you'll be better equipped to manage your emotional responses, even in the face of adversity.

- **Exercise 1 - Practice Mindfulness:** Engage in mindfulness meditation to stay present and become more aware of your thoughts and emotions. This practice can help you regulate your emotions by grounding yourself in the here and now.
- **Exercise 2 - Foster Gratitude:** Keep a gratitude journal to reflect on the positive aspects of your life. Focusing on gratitude can help you build resilience by shifting your perspective toward positivity, even in challenging times.
- **Exercise 3 - Develop a Growth Mindset:** Cultivate a growth mindset by embracing challenges as opportunities for growth. This mindset fosters resilience by encouraging you to view setbacks as a chance to learn and improve.
- **Exercise 4 - Embrace Self-Compassion:** Practice self-compassion by treating yourself with the same kindness and care you'd offer a friend. This exercise helps you build resilience by strengthening your self-esteem and emotional regulation.

- **Exercise 5 - Cultivate Social Connections:** Nurture your social relationships by staying connected with friends and loved ones. Social support is a vital aspect of resilience, providing a network of emotional support during challenging times.

- **Exercise 6 - Develop Problem-Solving Skills**: Enhance your problem-solving abilities by breaking down challenges into manageable steps. This exercise empowers you to build resilience by equipping you with practical skills to navigate difficulties.

- **Exercise 7 - Set Realistic Goals:** Establish achievable goals that allow you to measure your progress and build resilience by experiencing a sense of accomplishment.

- **Exercise 8 - Engage in Physical Activity**: Incorporate regular physical activity into your routine to boost your mental and emotional resilience. Exercise releases endorphins, which can help you manage stress and maintain emotional balance.

- **Exercise 9- Maintain a Resilience Journal**: Keep a resilience journal to document your experiences, emotions, and how you've coped with challenges. This exercise encourages self-reflection and growth, ultimately strengthening your resilience.

- **Exercise 10 - Seek Professional Support:** Don't hesitate to seek support from a mental health professional if you are facing significant challenges. Professional guidance can provide valuable tools and strategies to enhance your resilience.

As you embark on your journey to building resilience, remember that these exercises are like building blocks, each contributing to your emotional well-being and overall resilience. Over time, you'll find that these strategies empower you to face life's challenges with greater emotional regulation and a deeper understanding of your emotional response.

The journey to build resilience is not merely about bouncing back from adversity, it's about growing stronger through every experience. These resilience-building exercises serve as a foundation for enhancing your emotional regulation, fostering a positive outlook, and equipping you to navigate life's challenges with grace and fortitude. By building resilience, you're also deepening your emotional awareness and regulation, as both go hand in hand.

Now, let's transition into our next chapter, where we'll explore the intriguing world of integrating physical wellness into the recovery process. We'll dive into what it means to balance the link between the mind and body to increase our ability to heal from trauma and thrive in life. This chapter promises to equip you with powerful skills for enhancing your emotional and physical health, with exercise and nutrition to promote your overall well-being.

3

INTEGRATING PHYSICAL WELLNESS INTO YOUR RECOVERY PROCESS

All emotions, even those that are suppressed and unexpressed, have physical effects. Unexpressed emotions tend to stay in the body like small ticking time bombs- they are illnesses in incubation.

— MARILYN VAN M. DERBUR

The intricate link between your mind and body highlights how you can promote trauma recovery by nurturing your physical well-being. Our goal is to provide you with insights and strategies that underscore the profound connection between emotional healing and physical wellness. The above quote by Marilyn Van M. Derbur poignantly illustrates the undeniable connection between our emotions and physical well-being. It serves as a powerful reminder that our mental and emotional states are not isolated from our bodies; instead, they have a profound impact on our physical health.

In this chapter, we will explore this intricate relationship, uncover how unexpressed emotions affect our bodies, and provide you with practical guidance on how to nurture your physical wellness as an integral part of your trauma recovery journey. The mind-body connection is a dynamic and fascinating realm. By the end of this chapter, you'll have a deeper understanding of how to harness its potential for healing and resilience.

PHYSICAL EXERCISE

The mind and body are profoundly interconnected. Our physical well-being has a significant impact on our mental and emotional health, and this relationship becomes even more critical when dealing with trauma. We will, therefore, explore the remarkable role of physical exercises in trauma recovery. We'll examine how exercise can aid the healing process, supported by research findings and real-life stories. Additionally, we'll address common barriers to physical activity and provide strategies for staying motivated to move. Moreover, we'll introduce a range of fitness exercises and stretches designed to support your trauma recovery journey, including the practice of trauma-release exercises.

How Exercise Can Aid in Trauma Recovery

A physical exercise routine is a powerful tool in the process of trauma recovery. It acts as a bridge between the mind and the body, offering a holistic approach to healing. By engaging in regular physical activity, you can experience various benefits that contribute to your recovery.

- **Stress Reduction.** Exercise releases endorphins, often referred to as "feel-good" hormones, which help alleviate stress and boost mood. These positive effects are particularly beneficial for coping in the aftermath of traumatic experiences.
- **Improved Sleep.** Trauma can disrupt sleep patterns, leading to insomnia or nightmares. Exercise can help regulate sleep, enabling you to enjoy better rest and recovery.
- **Emotional Regulation.** Engaging in physical activity helps you manage your emotional responses more effectively. It provides a healthy outlet for pent-up emotions and empowers you to regain control over your emotional states.
- **Enhanced Self-Esteem.** Accomplishing physical fitness goals can boost self-esteem and self-efficacy, helping you regain your sense of agency and empowerment.
- **Mind-Body Connection.** Physical exercise strengthens the connection between the mind and

the body, fostering a greater awareness of physical sensations and emotions.

- **Stress Resilience.** Exercise helps you become more resilient to stressors by improving your physical health and emotional well-being.
- **Social Interactions.** Participating in group exercise activities can foster a sense of belonging and social support, which is essential in trauma recovery.

Research Findings

Numerous studies have highlighted the positive impact of exercise on trauma recovery:

- A study by the Trauma Incident Reduction Association (Greenwald, 2021) found that regular physical activity can significantly improve mental well-being after traumatic events.
- Research published in the Journal of Traumatic Stress in their study on the Relationship between physical activity and individual mental health after traumatic events (Wang et al., 2023) revealed that exercise helps you recover from trauma-related distress, with a notable reduction in symptoms such as flashbacks and nightmares.
- The Australian Centre of Posttraumatic Mental Health (*PTSD Awareness Day 2023 | EML*, n.d.) reported the benefits of exercise in supporting post-traumatic stress disorder (PTSD), emphasizing its

role in emotional regulation and reducing symptom severity.

- A study published in 2 Minute Medicine (Hing & Bhangu, 2021) emphasized the mental well-being improvements that result from physical activity after traumatic events.

Let's explore how physical exercise has been instrumental in one individual's trauma recovery journey.

A COMPELLING STORY OF TRAUMA RECOVERY THROUGH EXERCISE

Sarah, a survivor of a traumatic event, found herself facing severe anxiety and depression. Overwhelmed by the weight of her experiences, she felt trapped in a cycle of despair. During a therapy session, Sarah learned about the potential benefits of exercise in trauma recovery. She began her journey with simple steps - daily walks in the park. As she felt the warmth of the sun on her skin and observed the beauty of nature, a sense of serenity gradually crept in. These walks evolved into jogging and regular visits to a nearby gym.

Weightlifting became Sarah's refuge. She started with light weights and slowly progressed to heavier ones. Through each lift, she felt a release of the emotional burdens she had carried for so long. Sarah discovered that the act of lifting weights provided a sense of control that she had been missing. She was no longer helpless; she was strong. As she continued to exercise, Sarah noticed her anxiety decreasing and her mood improving. She began to sleep better, and her confidence grew. The gym became a space where she could confront her fears, challenge her limitations, and emerge stronger each day.

Sarah's story exemplifies the transformative power of exercise in trauma recovery. It is a testament to the resilience of the human spirit and the healing potential that physical activity offers. By taking that first step and gradually building her physical strength, Sarah found the emotional strength she needed to overcome the trauma that once held her captive.

Physical exercise is a vital component of trauma recovery, offering numerous benefits to those who have experienced trauma. Research studies highlight the positive impact of exercise on mental well-being, while real-life stories like Sarah's inspire us to harness the healing power of physical activity. As a holistic approach to recovery, exercise can help you rebuild your life, regain a sense of control, and find hope on your path to healing.

COMMON BARRIERS TO PHYSICAL ACTIVITY

Recognizing and addressing the barriers to physical activity is crucial for you on your trauma recovery journey. Some common barriers include:

- **Lack of Time:** One of the most common barriers is the perception of not having enough time for exercise. People often lead busy lives, juggling work, family, and other responsibilities.
- **Solution:** Prioritize physical activity by scheduling it into your daily or weekly routine. You don't need to spend hours at the gym; even short, high-intensity workouts can be effective. Find pockets of time throughout the day to stay active, such as taking short walks during breaks.
- **Low Motivation:** Motivation can wane, making it challenging to start or maintain an exercise routine.
- **Solution:** Establish clear and achievable fitness goals. Set short-term and long-term objectives to maintain motivation. Additionally, consider working out with a friend or hiring a personal trainer for added accountability and motivation.
- **Fatigue:** Feeling tired or overwhelmed can be a significant barrier to exercise.
- **Solution:** Choose exercises you enjoy and don't feel like a chore. Gentle activities like walking, yoga, or swimming can be rejuvenating. Listening to your body's needs and getting adequate rest is equally important.
- **Lack of Facilities of Equipment:** The absence of gym access or exercise equipment can deter many from physical activity.

- **Solution**: Bodyweight exercises require no equipment and can be done at home or in any open space. For strength training, you can use household items like water bottles or resistance bands to do stretches with the help of various websites available on the internet (YouTube and Trainerize.com). If you are new to exercise and strength, training consider starting with chair exercise routines or yoga for beginners. Outdoor activities such as walking in nature, running, hiking, or biking also require minimal equipment and are also pivotal for grounding oneself.
- **Health Conditions:** When you struggle with certain health concerns, you may be hesitant to engage in physical activity.
- **Solution:** Consult a healthcare professional before starting a new exercise routine, especially if you have pre-existing health conditions. They can recommend safe activities and provide guidance on managing any health issues while staying active.
- **Weather Conditions:** Unfavorable weather can discourage outdoor activities.
- **Solution:** Plan indoor exercises for days with poor weather. Indoor cycling, dancing, or home workouts are great alternatives. On better days, consider braving the elements or exploring activities that can be enjoyed in different weather conditions.

- **Social Isolation:** You may feel alone in your fitness journey, which can be demotivating.
- **Solution:** Join group exercise classes or virtual fitness communities. Exercising with friends or family, even if remotely, can provide a sense of camaraderie and support.
- **Self-Consciousness:** Fear of being judged or feeling self-conscious can hinder participation in group activities or gym settings.
- **Solution:** Remember that everyone starts somewhere, and improvement is a journey. Focus on personal progress rather than comparisons with others. Over time, self-confidence typically grows as fitness levels improve.

HOW TO STAY MOTIVATED TO MOVE

Maintaining motivation to exercise is a common challenge. Here are self-motivation tips to stay active:

- **Set Clear Goals:** Establish specific, achievable fitness goals. This provides a sense of purpose and direction in your exercise routine. Tracking your progress can be motivating.
- **Create a Routine:** Consistency is key. Make exercises a habitual part of your daily or weekly schedule. Over time, it becomes a natural and non-negotiable part of your day.

- **Vary Your Activities**: Prevent boredom by trying different types of exercise. Experiment with activities that you enjoy to keep things fresh and exciting. Variety keeps exercise interesting and fun.
- **Get an Exercise Buddy:** Sharing your fitness journey with someone can boost motivation and provide accountability. You're more likely to stick to your routine if someone else is counting on you.
- **Reward Yourself:** Set up a reward system for achieving your fitness goals. Treat yourself to something enjoyable or a special treat after reaching specific milestones.
- **Visualize Success**: Imagine the benefits of regular exercise, such as improved health, increased energy, and a better mood. Visualizing the positive outcomes can enhance motivation.
- **Remind Yourself Why**: Reflect on why you started exercising in the first place. Keep in mind the physical and emotional benefits that motivate you to embark on your fitness journey.
- **Track Your Progress:** Use a fitness app, journal, or calendar to record your workouts and achievements. Seeing your progress can be highly motivating.

Recognizing and addressing common barriers to physical activity and staying motivated are crucial steps in maintaining an active lifestyle. By implementing strategies to overcome these barriers and utilizing self-motivation tips, you can reap regular exercise's physical and emotional rewards, ultimately enhancing your overall well-being.

Exploring Effective Fitness Exercises and Routines for Trauma Recovery

Physical activity is a powerful trauma recovery tool, promoting physical and emotional healing. In this comprehensive exploration, we will delve into a variety of fitness exercises and routines that are particularly beneficial for you on your journey to recovery. These exercises not only contribute to physical well-being but also address emotional healing, providing a holistic approach to trauma recovery.

Balancing Activities:

- **Exercise Description**: Balancing activities involve challenging your balance and proprioception, which is the awareness of our body's position in space. A simple exercise involves standing on one leg while raising your arms to chest level or above, possibly holding extra weight for added resistance.
- **Benefits:** These exercises enhance core stability, coordination, and proprioception, helping you feel more in control of your body.
- **Tips:** To make it more challenging, try closing your eyes while balancing, further stimulating your proprioception and core engagement.

Contralateral Movements:

- **Exercise Description:** Contralateral movements engage both sides of the body simultaneously, such as crawling on all fours or performing single-leg deadlifts where one arm and the opposite leg work together.
- **Benefits:** These movements enhance coordination, balance, and cognitive function. They promote the integration of both brain hemispheres, which is crucial for emotional healing.
- **Tips**: Start with slow, controlled movements to ensure proper form. Gradually increase the complexity and intensity of these exercises.

Crossing Over the Midline:

- **Exercise Description:** Activities involving crossing over the midline of the body, such as Russian twists, are highly effective core exercises. This can be done by sitting on the floor and twisting your torso to touch the ground beside you. Curtsy lunges involve a variation of lunges where one leg crosses behind the other while lowering your body and returning to an upright position, this engages both body hemispheres by improving your stability, improving your overall ability to balance yourself, and improving your overall coordination while strengthening your muscles.

- **Benefits:** These exercises enhance coordination and cognitive function. Crossing the midline can stimulate brain activity and emotional processing.
- **Tips:** Start with low-intensity movements and gradually progress. Proper form is essential to avoid injury.

Strength and Mobility Work for the Posterior Chain and Core:

- **Exercise Description:** Engaging the posterior chain and core is essential for overall strength and stability. Exercises like rowing and deadlifting target these areas effectively.
- **Benefits**: These exercises help build strength, stability, and posture. A strong core is crucial for physical well-being and emotional resilience.
- **Tips:** When performing these exercises, focus on proper form and start with a weight or resistance level that is comfortable for your current fitness level.

Primal and Functional Movement Patterns:

- **Exercise Description**: These patterns include squatting, lunging, pushing, pulling, twisting, bending, walking, crawling, and running. They mimic natural, everyday movements.

- **Benefits:** Primal and functional movements improve overall strength, flexibility, and mobility. They also enhance functional fitness, making daily tasks easier.
- **Tips:** Start with basic movements and gradually progress to more complex patterns. Proper form and technique are essential for preventing injuries.

Neurogenic Yoga:

- **Exercise Description:** Neurogenic Yoga is a trauma-informed practice that combines gentle yoga poses, self-induced therapeutic tremors, and relaxation techniques.
- **Benefits:** This practice helps release tension, stress, and trauma stored in the body. It encourages emotional processing and provides a sense of relaxation and well-being.
- **Tips:** When exploring Neurogenic Yoga, follow a guided program or consider attending classes led by a qualified instructor.

Trauma-Release Exercises

Trauma-release exercises are designed to help you release emotional and physical tension stored in your body. These exercises can be valuable components of a trauma recovery routine. Here are some trauma release exercises you can try:

- Practice deep, diaphragmatic breathing to calm your nervous system and release tension. Deep breathing and breath control help increase focus and reduce anxiety.
- Try self-massage and trigger point release. Gently massaging areas of tension in your body can help release stored emotions. Focus on areas like your neck, shoulders, and back.
- Incorporate gentle stretching exercises to release physical tension and enhance flexibility. Yoga and Pilates are excellent options.
- Engage in grounding exercises, such as connecting with nature or focusing on your senses, to help you stay present and release emotional tension.
- Similar to Neurogenic Yoga, these exercises involve allowing the body to naturally tremor and release stored stress and trauma.
- Mindfulness Meditation: Mindfulness practices can help you become more aware of your emotions and physical sensations, leading to emotional release.

Stretches

Stretching exercises play a crucial role in promoting flexibility and reducing physical tension. Incorporate stretches that target areas of your body that tend to hold tension. This can include stretches for the neck, shoulders, back, hips, and legs. Stretching should be gentle and gradual to avoid overexertion.

Tremoring Exercise

A tremoring exercise is a practice that involves allowing the body to naturally tremor and release built-up physical tension. It can be an effective way to release stress, trauma, and pent-up emotions. One simple tremoring exercise you can try involves the following steps:

- Choose a quiet and comfortable space where you can sit or lie down. It's essential that you feel safe and free from distractions.
- Begin by taking a few deep breaths to relax and center yourself. Inhale deeply through your nose, and exhale slowly through your mouth. Focus on each breath, bringing your attention to the present moment.
- Set an intention for the exercise. It could be to release physical tension, reduce stress, or simply allow your body to move naturally.
- Gently start moving your body in a way that feels natural. You can begin by gently shaking your hands, fingers, or feet. Let the movements be spontaneous and fluid. Don't force anything; allow your body to guide you.
- If you feel comfortable, you can close your eyes to help you focus more on the internal sensation and less on the external environment.
- The key to tremoring exercises is letting go of control. Allow your body to move, shake, or tremor

as it wishes. This can be a gentle, almost imperceptible tremor or more pronounced shaking. Trust your body's innate wisdom.

- As you tremble, stay present and aware of any sensations that arise. Pay attention to how your body feels and any emotions or memories that may surface. The process may be accompanied by emotional releases, such as crying or laughter, which is entirely normal.

- You can continue this practice for as long as it feels comfortable. Some individuals may tremor for just a few minutes, while others may continue longer. Listen to your body and stop when you're ready.

- To conclude the exercise, gradually slow down your movements and come to a still position. Take a few deep breaths and express gratitude for this experience.

- After the exercise, take a moment to reflect on how you feel. Notice if there's any change in your physical and emotional state. This reflection can help you gain insights into the effects of the exercise.

It's important to note that a tremoring exercise can bring up strong emotions or memories. If you find the process challenging or overwhelming, consider seeking guidance from a therapist or counselor who specializes in trauma recovery. They can provide support and create a safe space for you to explore this technique. Remember that tremoring exercises can be a highly personal and individual experience. The goal is not to achieve a specific outcome but to allow your body to release tension and promote emotional well-being naturally.

Nutrition

Nutrition is a fundamental factor in trauma recovery, impacting both physical and mental well-being. The connection between what we eat and our ability to heal from trauma is profound and multifaceted. To understand this link, let's explore the key aspects that demonstrate how nutrition plays a pivotal role in trauma recovery. The brain relies on specific nutrients to produce neurotransmitters responsible for regulating mood and emotions. A diet rich in these nutrients, such as amino acids from lean proteins and complex carbohydrates from whole grains and fruits, can support the production of these crucial brain chemicals, potentially improving mood and emotional well-being.

Chronic inflammation in the body is associated with various mental health conditions. By adopting an anti-inflammatory diet, which includes foods like berries, leafy greens, and fatty fish rich in omega-3 fatty acids, it's possible to reduce inflammation and positively affect emotional well-being. The gut and the brain are intimately connected, and a healthy gut is closely linked to improved mood and emotional resilience. By including probiotic-rich foods like yogurt and sauerkraut in your diet, you can support your gut health and, in turn, your mental well-being.

Adequate nutrition provides the energy necessary for daily activities, including therapy sessions and self-care practices. A balanced diet can improve motivation and overall well-being, helping you better engage in the recovery process. Proper nutrition can enhance the body's ability to manage stress. Nutrient-dense food provides the necessary support for stress resilience, potentially reducing the impact of traumatic stress on mental health. Understanding what to include in your diet and what to avoid can significantly impact your trauma recovery journey:

Food to Include

- **Lean Proteins:** Lean protein is low-fat, high-protein food such as poultry, fish, tofu, or legumes, which can support neurotransmitter production and act like brain food, which can positively affect mood and emotional well-being and promote your heart health.
- **Complex Carbohydrates**: Whole grains, fruits, and vegetables offer sustained energy and support serotonin production, contributing to emotional stability.
- **Omega-3 Fatty Acids**: Fatty fish like salmon, flaxseeds, and walnuts are rich in omega-3 fatty acids, known for their anti-inflammatory properties and positive impact on cognitive function.
- **Antioxidant-Rich-Foods**: Berries, leafy grans, and colorful vegetables are packed with antioxidants that combat inflammation and oxidative stress.

- **Probiotic Foods**: Incorporating yogurt, kefir, or sauerkraut can support gut health, promoting a healthy gut-brain connection and, consequently, improved mental well-being.

Foods to Avoid

- **Processed Foods**: Limit processed foods high in added sugars, unhealthy fats, and artificial additives, as they can contribute to inflammation and mood swings.
- **Excessive Caffeine:** While moderate caffeine consumption is acceptable, excessive caffeine can disrupt sleep patterns and exacerbate anxiety.
- **Alcohol:** Excessive alcohol intake can negatively affect mood and emotional well-being.
- **High Sugar Intake**: A high sugar intake can lead to blood sugar spikes and crashes, affecting mood stability. Reducing sugar intake can help maintain balanced energy levels.

TRAUMA RECOVERY DIET

Incorporating the following tips into your dietary habits can support trauma recovery:

- Plan balanced meals and snacks in advance for the day, ensuring you get the necessary nutrients.

- Stay hydrated by drinking plenty of water to maintain mood and cognitive function.
- Practice mindful eating by paying attention to your food and how it makes you feel. Notice the smell, texture, and taste while you chew slowly to observe your sensations while eating. This can help you to identify any emotional connections to certain foods and identify the mood food you turn to in certain situations.
- Be mindful of emotional eating patterns and seek alternative coping mechanisms, such as talking to a therapist or practicing relaxation techniques.
- Consider consulting a registered dietitian or nutritionist, especially if you have specific dietary concerns or restrictions.
- Continuously educate yourself about the link between nutrition and mental health. Understanding the impact of your diet on emotional well-being empowers you to make healthier choices.
- Incorporate a wide variety of foods into your diet to ensure you receive a broad spectrum of nutrients.

Nutrition plays a vital role in trauma recovery by influencing brain chemistry, reducing inflammation, and promoting overall well-being. A diet of nutrient-dense foods, along with a mindful and balanced approach to eating, can be a valuable component of your healing journey. For personalized dietary advice that suits your specific needs and complements your trauma recovery process, always consult with a healthcare professional.

Somatic Therapy

The path to trauma recovery often involves a profound connection between the mind and body. Somatic therapy, a holistic approach to healing, offers a unique perspective on addressing psychological trauma by recognizing the vital role the body plays in this process. In this exploration, we will step into the world of somatic therapy, including its core concepts, techniques, types, and how this approach can help you on your trauma recovery journey.

Somatic therapy is a holistic approach to healing that focuses on the connection between the mind and body. It recognizes that emotional and psychological trauma often manifests physically in the body and aims to address this interconnectedness. Somatic therapy emphasizes that emotional experiences, memories, and traumatic events are not solely stored in the mind but can also be imprinted within the body.

This therapy seeks to uncover and release these somatic imprints, helping you process and heal from psychological trauma by addressing the physical manifestations of trauma stored deep within your mind and body. Somatic therapy aims to promote holistic well-being by releasing traumatic memories and improving emotional regulation and resilience, making use of touch and movement therapy.

Somatic therapy operates on the principle that the body, like the mind, retains memories and emotional experiences. When an individual experiences trauma, the body may respond with various physical sensations, tension, or discomfort. Somatic therapy facilitates healing by guiding you to connect with your body and explore these sensations, ultimately releasing trapped emotions and achieving a sense of wholeness.

The process typically involves a somatic therapist assisting the individual in recognizing and addressing these physical sensations and emotions. Through mindful exploration, you can release long-held trauma and emotional pain, thus fostering emotional and psychological healing.

SOMATIC THERAPY TECHNIQUES

Some therapy employs a range of techniques designed to enhance body awareness, grounding pendulation, titration, sequencing, and resourcing. These techniques aim to create a safe and supportive environment for you to explore and heal from trauma.

- **Body Awareness:** Body awareness is a fundamental somatic technique that encourages you to connect with your bodily sensations, helping you become more attuned to your physical responses to trauma. You can gain insights into your emotional states and trigger points by developing a deeper understanding of these sensations.

- **Grounding:** Grounding techniques are crucial for bringing you back to the present moment. Trauma often causes dissociation and detachment from the body. Grounding practices, such as deep breathing or focusing on the senses, help you reestablish your connection with your body and surroundings.
- **Pendulation:** Pendulation is a concept where you learn to move between sensations of comfort and discomfort. By oscillating between these states, you can gradually process trauma in manageable increments, helping to prevent emotional overwhelm.
- **Titration:** Titration is a practice in somatic therapy that encourages you to approach your traumatic experiences in small, tolerable doses. This gentle, step-by-step approach allows you to process your trauma without retraumatization.
- **Sequencing:** Sequencing in somatic therapy involves guiding you through a structured process of identifying, experiencing, and releasing somatic imprints related to trauma. This method helps you process your experiences systematically.
- **Resourcing:** Resourcing refers to the techniques and tools you can use to self-regulate and manage your emotional states. Resourcing exercises can provide

emotional support and grounding during challenging moments.

TYPES OF SOMATIC THERAPY

Various types of somatic therapy have emerged, each offering unique approaches to healing through the mind-body connection. Some of the most notable types include:

- **Somatic Experiencing:** Somatic Experiencing, developed by Dr. Peter Levine, focuses on resolving the effects of trauma by facilitating the release of physical tension and promoting emotional regulation. This approach emphasizes the completion of the body's instinctual responses to traumatic experiences.
- **Eye Movement Desensitization and Reprocessing (EMDR):** This is a structured therapy designed to reduce the impact of traumatic memories by using bilateral stimulation. Bilateral stimulation is eye movements incorporating visual stimulus to help you follow the movement from side to side with your eyes. This approach aims to reduce your reprocessing response to traumatic memories and reduce your emotional reaction.
- **Hakomi:** Hakomi is a mindfulness-based somatic therapy combining body-centered techniques and experiential practices. It focuses on the connection

between body and mind and encourages you to explore your core beliefs and emotional patterns.

- **Sensorimotor Psychotherapy:** This therapy, developed by Dr. Pat Ogden, combines talk therapy with somatic techniques. It emphasizes the importance of the body in understanding and healing psychological trauma. By addressing physical manifestations of trauma, you can explore and process your experiences.
- **Neurosomatic Therapy:** Neurosomatic therapy focuses on the relationship between the nervous system and the body. This approach aims to alleviate chronic pain and physical discomfort by addressing underlying neurological and somatic issues.

Each of these somatic therapy types offers a unique lens through which you can explore your mind-body connection, ultimately aiding in the healing process. The choice of which type to pursue may depend on an individual's specific needs and preferences.

Somatic therapy recognizes the profound connection between the mind and body, offering a holistic approach to trauma recovery. By addressing the physical manifestations of trauma and fostering body awareness, somatic therapy empowers you to release trapped emotions and find healing. With these various techniques and types of somatic therapy available, you can choose the approach that best suits your needs and embark on a transformative journey toward holistic well-being.

ACUPUNCTURE

Acupuncture, a millennia-old practice rooted in Traditional Chinese Medicine (TCM), is an alternative therapy to relieve the body from pain and stored trauma causing anxiety, arthritis, or depression symptoms. It involves the practitioner inserting thin needles into specific points on the body, known as acupoints and is mapped according to your unique symptoms, injury or pain points. These acupoints are believed to correspond to various bodily functions, organs, and emotions. Acupuncture aims to balance the body's energy, or qi (pronounced "chee"), and promote holistic well-being.

Acupuncture works on the principle of rebalancing the body's energy flow. In TCM, it is believed that disruptions in the flow of qi can lead to emotional imbalances, manifesting as anxiety, depression, and other emotional pain. By inserting needles into acupoints, acupuncture practitioners aim to clear blockages and restore the free flow of qi, thereby alleviating emotional distress.

Emotional pain often manifests as physical tension and discomfort, and acupuncture recognizes the mind-body connection. The practice can address both the emotional and physical aspects of trauma by releasing endorphins, the body's natural painkillers, and mood boosters, which can provide emotional relief. Acupuncture has been shown to reduce stress and anxiety, making it a valuable tool for your recovery from trauma. The calming effect of acupuncture sessions can help you relax, restore emotional balance, and find relief from emotional pain.

Various studies have explored the effectiveness of acupuncture in addressing emotional pain. One study published in JAMA International Medicine (Yin et al., 2022) found that acupuncture significantly reduces the severity of depressive symptoms. Additionally, research published in the Journal of Endocrinology (Eshkevari et al., 2013) revealed that acupuncture could regulate the release of stress hormones and influence emotional responses positively.

Acupuncture is a holistic approach that views the body and mind as interconnected. This perspective is invaluable for seeking emotional recovery, as it acknowledges the profound connection between psychological and physical well-being.

ACUPRESSURE

Acupressure is a technique closely related to acupuncture but does not involve needles. Instead, a utilized manual pressure is applied to acupoints on the body to promote healing and well-being.

Here's how acupressure can aid in emotional recovery:

- Acupressure focuses on specific acupoints known for your emotional release properties. By applying pressure to these points, you can release trapped emotions and tension, offering a sense of relief.
- Acupressure can be a valuable tool for addressing childhood traumas. Some acupressure points are believed to be connected to early emotional experiences. Gently stimulating these points can help you process and release unresolved childhood traumas.
- Like acupuncture, acupressure can reduce stress and anxiety by promoting relaxation and regulating the body's response to emotional triggers.
- Acupressure is a self-help technique that allows you to practice it on your own. By learning the acupressure points related to emotional release, you can have a valuable tool for self-care and emotional recovery.

Interactive Element: 30-Day Healthy Body Healthy Mind Challenge

As we explore the benefits of acupuncture and acupressure, let's embark on a 30-day challenge to harmonize our body and mind. This challenge is designed to align with the content and recommendations of this chapter, promoting emotional well-being through holistic practices.

Week 1: Introduction to Acupuncture and Acupressure

Day 1-7: Start with an introduction to acupuncture and acupressure. Learn about the acupoints related to emotional release and practice basic acupressure techniques for relaxation.

Week 2: Dive Deeper into Acupressure

Day 8-14: Explore acupressure techniques for specific emotional issues. Focus on releasing emotional pain, stress reduction, and processing past traumas.

Week 3: Self-Healing with Acupressure

Day 15-21: Dive into self-healing with acupressure. Create a daily routine that includes acupressure practices to maintain emotional balance and well-being.

Week 4: Acupuncture Session

Consider scheduling an acupuncture session with a licensed practitioner—experience firsthand the potential benefits of acupuncture in reducing emotional pain and promoting holistic well-being.

In the upcoming chapter, we'll explore the way to trauma recovery, making use of mindfulness and self-care strategies. Just as acupuncture and acupressure address the mind-body connection, nutrition plays a pivotal role in healing and emotional well-being. These two aspects are carrying us further on our healing journey. Join us in discovering how mindfulness and self-care can impact our emotional journey to recovery.

4

FINDING CALM AMIDST CHAOS: MINDFULNESS AND SELF-CARE STRATEGIES IN TRAUMA RECOVERY

Trauma doesn't disappear when you ignore it.

— STEPHANIE M. HUTCHINS

Trauma has a way of lingering, quietly affecting our lives even when we attempt to ignore it. But as Stephanie M. Hutchins reminds us, its presence can cast a shadow on our daily experiences, leaving us grappling with the past and uncertain about the future. In these moments, we often yearn for a sanctuary, a place where we can find solace, courage, and healing. Mindfulness and self-care strategies unveil your transformative power within the refuge of the present.

In the following pages, we will explore various mindfulness techniques and self-care practices that will help you navigate the tumultuous waters of trauma recovery. Together, we will discover how the power of the present moment can heal the past and shape a more compassionate, resilient future.

WHAT THE SCIENCE SAYS

The efficacy of mindfulness in trauma recovery is not a mere abstraction but rather a well-documented and scientifically supported path toward healing and resilience. Research has shown that mindfulness practices offer a profound opportunity for you to regain control over your emotional well-being and reclaim a sense of calm amidst the chaos of trauma. Let's discover the findings of scientific studies and research together that underscore the effectiveness of mindfulness in aiding trauma recovery.

The U.S. Department of Veterans Affairs (VA) emphasizes in its study (*Treatment Essentials*, n.d.) that mindfulness is a valuable component in the treatment of trauma, particularly Post-Traumatic Stress Disorder (PTSD). According to their research and clinical practice guidelines, mindfulness-based interventions contribute significantly to trauma recovery. These interventions, which include Mindfulness-Based Stress Reduction (MBRS) and Mindfulness-Based Cognitive Therapy (MBCT), have been shown to reduce the severity of PTSD symptoms and improve overall well-being. The VA's endorsement is a testament to the robust scientific backing for mindfulness in trauma recovery.

Researchers have recognized the need for comprehensive approaches to trauma recovery in high-violence, low-resource settings. The study "The Case for Mindfulness Interventions for Traumatic Stress in High-Violence, Low-Resource Settings"(Pillay & Eagle, 2021) highlights the potential of mindfulness in such challenging contexts. It underscores that mindfulness-based interventions can be cost-effective and accessible tools to address trauma-related issues, such as anxiety, depression, and emotional dysregulation.

Neuroscientific studies provide a deeper understanding of how mindfulness affects the brain and contributes to trauma recovery. Research published in the National Center of Biotechnology Information (NCBI) (Boyd et al., 2018) delves into the neural mechanism that underlies the benefits of mindfulness in trauma therapy. It discusses how mindfulness practices can alter the brain's structure and functions, impacting areas related to emotional regulation, memory, and self-awareness.

Mindfulness offers a holistic approach to trauma recovery, addressing the emotional, psychological, and physical dimensions of trauma. Research conducted by the National Center for PTSD (*PTSD: National Center for PTSD*, n.d.) consistently shows that mindfulness practices reduce trauma symptoms, including intrusive thoughts, avoidance behavior, and hypervigilance. This approach allows you to regain control over your responses to traumatic triggers and experience a greater sense of emotional regulation.

Therefore, studies confirm the clinical utility of mindfulness-based interventions in trauma therapy. They have been shown to improve overall functioning, decrease depression and anxiety symptoms, and enhance the quality of life for trauma survivors. Such research underscores that mindfulness is not just a complementary approach but an integral aspect of trauma recovery.

Trauma-Informed Mindfulness

Trauma-informed mindfulness is a therapeutic approach that recognizes the profound impact of trauma on your well-being and seeks to promote healing and resilience through the practice of mindfulness. Unlike conventional mindfulness, which may not always be safe for trauma survivors, trauma-informed mindfulness is a carefully crafted framework designed to create a secure space for trauma survivors to explore their inner landscapes and find solace amidst their experiences.

What is trauma-informed mindfulness, and how does it differ from traditional mindfulness practices? Trauma-informed mindfulness is an approach rooted in deep understanding and compassion for the experiences of trauma survivors. It acknowledges the inherent vulnerabilities and sensitivities that trauma can create and tailors mindfulness practices to address these unique needs. The overarching goal of trauma-involved mindfulness is to provide a safe, nurturing space for you to engage with your experiences, allowing them to begin the journey of healing.

Trauma-informed mindfulness recognizes that trauma is not just a mental experience; it is a full-body, all-encompassing ordeal. This perspective sees trauma survivors as those who have experienced a deep sense of unsafety, a feeling that often extends to their bodies. This is a critical aspect to understand when differentiating trauma-informed mindfulness from conventional mindfulness.

Trauma-informed mindfulness practices are grounded in the principles of practicing mindfulness in a safe environment creating a sense of safety and with self-compassion and respect toward yourself and others. It provides a sense of safety, choice, collaboration, trustworthiness, and empowerment while recognizing one's traumatic memories without a sense of overwhelming emotional distress. These principles form the foundation of trauma-informed care, emphasizing the importance of creating environments and practices that prioritize a survivor's sense of security and control.

The Perils of Uninformed Mindfulness

Mindfulness, a practice aimed at bringing one's attention to the present moment without judgment, can be a potent tool for emotional healing. However, it is crucial to recognize that conventional mindfulness practices may not always be safe for trauma survivors. In the absence of trauma-informed guidelines, those who have experienced trauma may find that mindfulness unintentionally triggers distressing memories or overwhelming emotions, potentially exacerbating their suffering.

Trauma survivors often live with persistent emotional and physical reactions to traumatic experiences. These reactions can manifest as hypervigilance, dissociation, anxiety, or depression. In the presence of these symptoms, practicing conventional mindfulness can be overwhelming, as it may expose trauma survivors to sensations, emotions, and thoughts they are not yet ready to confront.

For example, a survivor of a car accident may have intrusive thoughts about the accident while practicing mindfulness. The sudden surfacing of this memory may trigger intense anxiety, making you feel unsafe and potentially leading to re-traumatization.

Uninformed mindfulness may also inadvertently replicate power dynamics. When you are encouraged to let go of your thoughts and just "be in the moment," it might inadvertently feel like a dismissal of your traumatic experiences and the significance of your distress. This can lead to a sense of being unheard or invalidated, which is counterproductive to the healing process.

HOW TO SAFELY USE MINDFULNESS FOR TRAUMA

To safely utilize mindfulness as a trauma survivor, it is vital to adopt a trauma-informed approach. This entails conscious modifications to mindfulness practices to ensure they do not unintentionally activate traumatic responses. As individuals explore their internal landscapes, it is essential to proceed with caution, respecting the unique needs and boundaries that trauma survivors bring to their practice.

Trauma-informed mindfulness recognizes the importance of establishing a safe and nurturing environment for survivors to embark on their healing journey. While mindfulness can be a potent tool, it must be introduced in a manner that prioritizes safety and emotional regulation. Here are key components to consider when initiating trauma-informed mindfulness:

- **Formal Practice:** Formal mindfulness practices are structured exercises that guide you through becoming aware of the present moment. Trauma survivors can benefit from these practices when adapted to their unique needs. Formal practices may include body scans, loving-kindness meditation, or breath awareness. These practices often begin with an invitation to cultivate a sense of safety. This may involve grounding techniques, such as feeling the support of the chair or the ground beneath, to help you become anchored in the present.

- **Informal Practice:** In addition to formal practices, trauma-informed mindfulness encourages the integration of mindfulness into daily life. This informal practice emphasizes the cultivation of a constant state of awareness. It is not just about the moments spent in meditation but also about extending mindfulness into daily activities. Trauma survivors can practice mindful eating, walking, or simply observing the world around them with a sense of curiosity and self-compassion.

GUIDELINES AND BEST PRACTICES

Trauma-informed mindfulness relies on a set of guidelines and best practices that prioritize safety, emotional regulation, and self-compassion. These guidelines include:

- A safe space is critical for trauma survivors. The environment where mindfulness practices occur should be calming, free of distractions, and void of any triggering stimuli. It should communicate a sense of security and control.
- Trauma-informed mindfulness emphasizes self-compassion. Survivors are encouraged to approach their experiences with kindness, recognizing that healing is gradual. Self-compassion includes being gentle with oneself and not forcing progress.

- Boundaries are essential to ensure that trauma survivors have agency over their practice. They can choose what to explore and avoid, and their boundaries should always be respected.
- Mindfulness practices for trauma survivors should proceed at a pace that is comfortable for them. Trauma-informed mindfulness recognizes that healing cannot be rushed and that it is essential to meet survivors where they are.

Exercises to Try for Trauma Recovery

Mindfulness exercises play a central role in trauma-informed mindfulness practices. These exercises offer a structured approach to cultivating present-moment awareness, self-compassion, and emotional regulation. They provide trauma survivors with practical tools to engage with their trauma experiences and the emotions they evoke. Some common mindfulness exercises in trauma-informed practices include:

- **Grounding Techniques:** These exercises involve engaging the senses to anchor oneself in the present moment. For example, trauma survivors may focus on the sensation of their feet on the ground, the texture of an object they are holding, or the sound of their breath. Grounding techniques help you feel connected to your body and the present moment, countering dissociation or hypervigilance.

- **Pendulation:** Pendulation is a core trauma healing tool that has proven successful when used during trauma therapy. In creating a balance between the arousal of traumatic triggers and the ability to remain calm among the pulsations of the nervous system during exposure to traumatic memories. It involves moving back and forth between feelings of safety and discomfort. Trauma survivors learn to navigate their emotional landscape gradually, oscillating between sensations that feel safe and those that are more challenging. This process helps build emotional regulation and resilience.

- **Titration:** Titration is the practice of breaking down overwhelming experiences into smaller, more manageable parts. After the smaller manageable parts are recognized, solutions to each step are considered until a final overall solution to the entire experience is reached. It involves acknowledging what one can handle at any given moment and not pushing too far beyond one's emotional capacity. Trauma survivors learn to approach their experiences in bite-sized portions, promoting emotional safety.

- **Sequencing:** Sequencing exercises help trauma survivors connect with their bodies and emotions through movement. Sequencing may include slow, gentle movements or progressive muscle relaxation. These exercises encourage survivors to explore the physical sensations associated with their emotions, promoting self-awareness and self-regulation.

- **Resourcing:** Resourcing exercises involve creating an emotional toolkit of positive memories or experiences. Trauma survivors learn to draw upon these resources during difficult moments, providing comfort and strength during their healing journey.

The journey of trauma recovery is deeply personal and unique to you. Trauma-informed mindfulness serves as a guiding light, offering a path towards healing and resilience.

Nurturing Resilience Through Self-Care

Self-care is often described as the practice of caring for oneself to maintain or improve well-being. In the context of trauma recovery, self-care plays a crucial role in promoting healing, emotional resilience, and overall mental health. Trauma survivors often face emotional and psychological challenges, and self-care can help them navigate these complex terrains effectively. Recognizing signs that indicate the need for more self-care is important on your journey.

The significance of self-care in trauma recovery cannot be overstated. Trauma survivors often endure immense psychological, emotional, and physical burdens. The aftermath of trauma can lead to a variety of challenges, including heightened stress, anxiety, depression, and a profound sense of vulnerability. Engaging in self-care practices can significantly mitigate these challenges and help you regain a sense of control and balance in your life.

Self-care encompasses a wide range of practices and activities that support emotional, mental, and physical well-being. It can include mindfulness, relaxation techniques, engaging in hobbies, physical exercise, maintaining a healthy diet, seeking therapy, practicing gratitude, setting boundaries, and much more. The precise self-care strategies that are effective may vary from person to person, emphasizing the importance of personalizing one's self-care plan.

SIGNS YOU NEED MORE SELF-CARE

Recognizing when you need more self-care is a fundamental aspect of trauma recovery. It is crucial to be attuned to your emotional and physical needs. Several signs may indicate that you require more self-care.

- Persistent stress can manifest as physical tension, emotional exhaustion, and a feeling of being overwhelmed. When stress levels rise, it's a clear indicator that self-care is needed.
- Emotional exhaustion can manifest as emptiness, irritability, or an inability to cope with daily challenges.
- Heightened anxiety can lead to racing thoughts, restlessness, and difficulty concentrating.

- A persistent lack of energy may indicate a need for more self-care. Fatigue can take a toll on both physical and emotional well-being.
- Physical symptoms, such as headaches, muscle tension, and digestive issues, can be physical manifestations of stress and a lack of self-care.
- Emotional sensitivity can lead to heightened emotional reactions to situations that were not previously distressing.
- Neglecting one's basic needs, such as sleep, nutrition, or personal hygiene, can be a clear sign of insufficient self-care.
- Difficulty falling asleep or staying asleep can be an indication of heightened stress and the need for self-care practices to promote relaxation.
- Feeling detached or disconnected from one's emotions and experiences can be a sign of emotional exhaustion.

ASKING THE RIGHT QUESTIONS

Understanding your self-care requires asking yourself the right questions. These inquiries can provide valuable insights into your unique self-care requirements. When considering self-care, it is beneficial to ask yourself:

- **Physical Self-Care**
- What physical activities make me feel most alive and energized?
- Am I getting adequate rest and quality sleep?
- How is my relationship with food, and am I maintaining a balanced diet?
- Do I incorporate regular physical exercise into my routine?
- **Emotional Self-Care**
- What brings me emotional comfort and joy?
- How do I cope with stress, and are those methods effective?
- Do I healthily express my emotions and thoughts?
- Am I seeking emotional support when needed, whether through friends, family, or therapy?

BUILDING A SELF-CARE PLAN

Constructing a self-care plan is an essential step in prioritizing one's emotional and mental health. A well-structured self-care plan can offer guidance and support for navigating the challenges of trauma recovery. Below, we will outline a step-by-step process for creating a personalized self-care plan:

- **Self-Reflection:** Begin by engaging in self-reflection. Consider what activities, practices, or routines genuinely nourish your well-being. Reflect on your strengths, preferences, and areas that need improvement.
- **Identify Key Needs:** Determine the areas of self-care that require attention. These may include physical health, emotional well-being, spiritual growth, relationships, or personal growth. Pinpoint the specific aspects you wish to address in your plan.
- **Set Realistic Goals**: Establish attainable self-care goals. Avoid overburdening yourself with an extensive list of activities. Start small and gradually expand your self-care practices.
- **Create a Schedule:** Incorporate self-care activities into your daily, weekly, or monthly schedule. Developing a structured routine ensures that self-care becomes an integral part of your life.
- **Seek Professional Guidance**: If necessary, consult healthcare professionals or therapists for guidance on creating an effective self-care plan. They can provide valuable insights and recommend activities specifically tailored to your needs.

- **Monitor Progress:** Regularly assess your self-care journey. Note the positive changes and adjustments you need to make in your plan. Adapt your self-care practices as needed to ensure they remain effective.

Self-Care Plan Template

For a structured approach to building your self-care plan, consider using the templates available at www.pitt.edu or follow the guide below. This template guides you through the essential steps of identifying your self-care needs, setting goals, and incorporating self-care practices into your life. Self-care is a potent tool for trauma survivors on their healing journey. By recognizing its importance, identifying signs that you need more self-care, and asking yourself the right questions, you can craft a self-care plan that nurtures your physical and emotional well-being. This plan empowers you to prioritize self-compassion and cultivate a sense of peace amid the chaos of trauma recovery. Creating a 30-day self-care plan for trauma healing:

Week 1: Cultivating Mindfulness and Awareness

- Day 1-7 Mindfulness Meditation
- Begin each day with a 10-minute mindfulness meditation to ground yourself.
- Focus on your breath and bodily sensations, practicing presence in the moment.

Week 2: Nurturing Emotional Well-Being

- Day 8-14 Journaling for Emotional Expression
- Continue with mindfulness meditation, set a time and add this exercise at another time of day.
- Dedicate 15 minutes each day to journaling your thoughts, emotions, and reflections.
- Explore your feelings, fears, and aspirations, allowing for emotional release.

Week 3: Physical Self-Care

- Day 15-21 Physical Activity and Nutrition
- Keep your routine with the above two exercises adding this to your routine.
- Engage in 30 minutes of light exercise, such as walking or yoga, each day.
- Incorporate more fruits, vegetables, and water into your diet for enhanced physical well-being.

Week 4: Creative Expression and Social Connection

- Day 22-30 Creative Expression and Reaching Out.
- Keep your routine as above and add one more step.
- Spend time on a creative activity, like drawing, writing, or playing music, for at least 20 minutes each day.

- Reconnect with a friend or family member, sharing your experiences and seeking social support.

This 30-day self-care plan is a gentle approach to healing from trauma, emphasizing mindfulness, emotional expression, physical well-being, creative outlets, and social connection. Adjust it to your specific needs, and remember that self-compassion is the key to your healing journey.

Self-Care Practices for Trauma Recovery

Trauma can have a profound impact on our physical and emotional health. As part of the journey to recovery, self-care is an essential component to foster resilience and promote healing. This section delves into a variety of self-care practices that can empower you to take control of your well-being, with a particular focus on the importance of restorative sleep and ways to achieve it.

GENERAL CATEGORIES OF SELF-CARE PRACTICES

To effectively address self-care in the context of trauma recovery, it's beneficial to categorize these practices into general groups, as highlighted in the resource Trauma Counseling—Self-Care After Trauma (Truitt, 2019).

These categories provide a structured approach to nurturing overall well-being:

- **Physical Self-Care:** This includes activities that focus on the physical aspects of well-being, such as exercise, nutrition, and restorative sleep.
- **Emotional Self-Care:** Emotional self-care creates a caring practice of the practice and techniques to help you manage your emotions and cope with stress effectively, with self-love as the key emotional focus. These may include therapy, meditation, or journaling.
- **Social Self-Care:** Building and maintaining healthy social connections are vital for trauma recovery. Social self-care practices encompass engaging with supportive friends and family and setting boundaries when needed.
- **Spiritual Self-Care:** For many, spiritual practices, meditation, or spending time in nature can be essential for healing and self-discovery.
- **Mental Self-Care**: Mental self-care focuses on maintaining cognitive health through daily activities to improve mental health. Activities such as puzzles, reading, or learning new skills can also be beneficial. With this technique, you promote self-care and increase your ability to manage your mood, emotions, and reactions effectively.

- **Creative Self-Care:** Engaging in creative activities, such as art, music, or writing, can provide an outlet for emotional expression and healing. Articulating your emotions through painting, writing, and dancing is an effective tool to use during the healing process as it opens the blank canvas allowing you to express yourself without judgment or restriction.

Restorative Sleep

One of the most fundamental aspects of self-care for trauma survivors is ensuring they receive restorative sleep. Restorative sleep differs from non-restorative sleep in that it allows the body and mind to truly heal, regenerate, and refresh. While non-restorative sleep may leave you feeling tired and fatigued, even after a full night's rest, restorative sleep is invigorating.

Understanding the importance of restorative sleep and how it differs from non-restorative sleep is essential in the context of trauma recovery. Restorative sleep plays a critical role in processing emotions and memories, which is particularly vital for those dealing with traumatic experiences.

A crucial function of restorative sleep is that it enables the brain to engage in activities that help process and make sense of emotions. Without restorative sleep, you are more likely to experience heightened stress, emotional distress, and a sense of overwhelm.

Scientific research emphasizes the importance of restorative sleep in trauma recovery. Articles such as The Stuff of Dreams: How Sleep Eases Emotional Trauma (ABC News, 2011) explore how dreams can ease the effects of trauma and post-traumatic stress disorder, highlighting the connection between sleep and emotional processing. Furthermore, Psychology Today, in their journal on *Trauma, Stress, and Restorative Sleep* (*Glauser*, 2012), provides insights into how trauma and stress can disrupt restorative sleep, underscoring its significance.

Achieving Restorative Sleep

- Ensure your sleeping space is comfortable, dark, and quiet. Investing in a comfortable mattress and pillows can significantly promote restful sleep.
- Try to maintain a consistent sleep schedule by going to bed and waking up at the same time each day, even on weekends. This consistency helps regulate your body's internal clock.
- The blue light emitted by phones, tablets, and computers can interfere with your ability to fall asleep. Avoid screens at least an hour before bedtime.
- Engage in relaxation practices before sleep, such as deep breathing, meditation, or gentle stretching exercises.
- Limit or avoid caffeine and nicotine, particularly in the hours leading up to bedtime.

- While alcohol may initially make you feel drowsy, it can disrupt your sleep cycle. Consume alcohol in moderation.
- Regular exercise can improve sleep quality. However, complete vigorous workouts at least a few hours before bedtime.
- Establish a soothing bedtime ritual, which may include reading, taking a warm bath, or practicing mindfulness.
- If you struggle with sleep issues related to trauma, consider consulting a mental health professional who can provide guidance and support.

Incorporating these strategies into your self-care routine can significantly enhance the quality of your sleep and, in turn, contribute to your overall well-being in the journey of trauma recovery. Restorative sleep is a fundamental aspect of self-care, and by understanding its importance and adopting healthy sleep habits, you can nurture your emotional and physical health as you work toward healing.

Sleep Hacks for More Restorative Sleep

Restorative sleep is an essential element of self-care, particularly for those on the path of trauma recovery. It provides the necessary space for the body and mind to heal and rejuvenate. While trauma may often lead to sleep disturbances, practicing sleep hacks can help improve the quality of sleep. In this section, we will explore 20 sleep hacks, discussing how to implement them and why they are effective based on valuable insights from resources found at Sleep Adviser—(Zwarensteyn, 2021) and the University of Colorado Boulder—(*7 Hacks for Better Sleep*, 2021).

Establish a Consistent Sleep Schedule

- **How to do it:** Set a regular bedtime and wake-up time, even on weekends, to regulate your body's internal clock.
- **Why it Works:** Consistency helps align your body's circadian rhythm, making it easier to fall asleep and wake up at the desired times.

Create a Comfortable Sleep Environment

- **How to do it:** Invest in a comfortable mattress and pillows. Ensure your bedroom is dark, quiet, and at a comfortable temperature.
- **Why it Works:** An ideal sleep environment promotes relaxation and minimizes disturbances that can disrupt restorative sleep.

Limit Exposure to Screens

- **How to do it:** Avoid screens at least an hour before bedtime, as the blue light emitted by phones, tablets, and computers can interfere with sleep.

- **Why it works:** Reducing exposure to screens helps you wind down, making it easier to fall asleep.

Relaxation Techniques

- **How to do it:** Engage in relaxation practices such as deep breathing, meditation, or gentle stretching exercises.
- **Why it works:** These techniques reduce stress and anxiety, creating an optimal mental state for restorative sleep.

Avoid Stimulants

- **How to do it:** Limit or avoid caffeine and nicotine, especially in the hours leading up to bedtime.
- **Why it works:** Stimulants disrupt your ability to fall asleep and can lead to sleep disturbances.

Limit Alcohol

- **How to do it:** Consume alcohol in moderation and avoid it at least a few hours before bedtime.
- **Why it works:** While alcohol may make you feel drowsy, it can negatively affect sleep quality.

Regular Physical Activity

- **How to do it**: Engage in regular exercise but complete workouts during the daytime and relaxation stretches at night.
- **Why it works:** Physical activity can promote better sleep quality by reducing stress and promoting relaxation.

Mindful Bedtime Routine

- **How to do it:** Establish a calming bedtime ritual, reading, taking a warm bath, practicing mindfulness, or relaxing meditation.
- **Why it works:** A bedtime routine signals to your body that it's time to wind down, making it easier to fall asleep.

Ensure a Comfortable Mattress and Pillow

- **How to do it:** Choose a mattress and pillows that offer the right support and comfort for your preferences. Focus on good back support.
- **Why it works:** An uncomfortable mattress or pillow can lead to physical discomfort and disrupt sleep.

Control Noise and Light

- **How to do it:** Use earplugs or white noise machines to block out the noise. Ensure your room is dark, or wear an eye mask if necessary.
- **Why it works:** Minimizing environmental disturbances can promote restorative sleep.

Maintain Optimal Room Temperature

- **How to do it:** Adjust the room temperature to a comfortable level, usually between 60-67F (15-20C).
- **Why it works:** An optimal room temperature ensures you're neither too hot nor too cold, which can disrupt sleep.

Manage Stress

- **How to do it:** Practice stress-reduction techniques such as meditation, mindfulness, or relaxation exercises.
- **Why it works:** Managing stress reduces anxiety and allows for a more restful night's sleep.

Limit Fluid Intake Before Bed

- **How to do it:** Reduce your liquid intake, particularly caffeine and alcohol, in the hours before bedtime.

- **Why it works:** Minimizing fluids helps prevent middle-of-the-night awakenings to use the bathroom.

Create a Sleep-Inducing Bedroom Atmosphere

- **How to do it:** Decorate your bedroom with soothing colors, comfortable bedding, and calming decor.
- **Why it works**: A sleep-inducing atmosphere can help your body recognize the bed as a place for rest.

Reserve Bed for Sleep

- **How to do it:** Avoid working, studying, or watching TV in bed. Reserve your bed exclusively for sleep.
- **Why it works:** This mental association helps your body recognize the bed as a place for rest.

Keep Electronics Out of the Bedroom

- **How to do it:** Remove television, computers, and smartphones from your bedroom.
- **Why it works:** Electronics can be stimulating and disrupt the sleep environment.

Avoid Heavy Meals Before Bed

- **How to do it:** Finish eating large or spicy meals at least a few hours before bedtime. Keep dinner time with lighter meals, and make lunchtime a large meal with heavy foods.
- **Why it works:** Heavy meals can cause discomfort and disrupt your ability to fall asleep.

Daylight Exposure

- **How to do it:** Spend time outdoors during the day to expose yourself to natural light.
- **Why it works:** Daylight exposure helps regulate your body's internal clock.

Bedtime Snacks

- **How to do it:** If you need a snack before bedtime, choose sleep-promoting options like warm milk, yogurt, or a banana.
- **Why it works:** Certain foods can encourage restorative sleep by containing sleep-inducing components.

Cognitive Behavioral Therapy for Insomnia (CBT-I)

- **How to do it:** Consider CBT-I, a structured program offered by a therapist to address insomnia.
- **Why it works:** CBT-I can be highly effective in treating insomnia and improving sleep quality.

Incorporating these sleep hacks into your routine can significantly enhance the quality of your sleep and promote restorative rest. While these hacks may vary in effectiveness from person to person, exploring and implementing the ones that work best for you can lead to improved sleep quality, which is crucial for overall well-being, especially during trauma recovery. A consistent practice of these strategies can profoundly impact the quality of your sleep, ultimately contributing to your emotional and physical healing.

In the pursuit of healing and resilience, we have journeyed through the intricate terrain of trauma recovery. The previous chapter guided us through exercises, mindfulness practices, and self-care strategies that empower us to heal and reconnect with our inner strength. As we continue exploring the multifaceted path toward recovery, we are now on the precipice of a new chapter that delves deep into spirituality. Chapter 5, "Harnessing Spirituality for Trauma Resilience," will transport us into the profound realm of the human spirit. It's here that we'll discover how spirituality can be a powerful ally in our journey to healing.

MAKE A DIFFERENCE WITH YOUR REVIEW

UNLOCK THE POWER OF KINDNESS

"Unless someone like you cares a whole awful lot, nothing is going to get better. It's not." - Dr. Seuss

People who help others without asking for anything in return live happier, longer lives. So if we've got a chance to do that here, I want to try!

I have a question for you...

Would you help someone you've never met, even if no one knew you did it?

Who is this mystery person, you ask? They are a lot like you. Or at least, how you used to be. Less experienced, wanting to get better, and needing help but not sure where to look.

My goal is to make healing from trauma easy for everyone to understand. Everything I do is based on that goal. And the only way I can meet that goal is by reaching...well...everyone!

This is where you come in. Most people do judge a book by its cover and reviews. So here is my ask on behalf of someone struggling that you have never met:

Please help them by writing this book a review.

Your gift costs no money and less than 60 seconds, but can change someone's life forever. Your review could help...

...one more person start their healing journey.
...one more person find hope.
...one more person feel less alone.

To get that "I helped someone!" feeling and really help them, all you have to do is...it takes less than 60 seconds...

Leave a review.

Just scan the code below to leave your review:

If you feel good about helping someone you can't see, you're my kind of person. Welcome to the club - you're one of us!

I'm even more excited to share the lessons in the next chapters that will help you heal faster and feel better than you can imagine. You'll love the tips I'm about to share.

Thank you from the bottom of my heart. Now, back to helping you!

- Your biggest fan, Sophia L. Ray

5

HARNESSING SPIRITUALITY FOR TRAUMA RESILIENCE

There's no weakness as great as false strength.

— STEFAN MOLYNEUX

In our pursuit of healing, we have explored the depths of our inner selves, seeking to mend the wounds left behind by trauma. We have delved into the power of self-care, mindfulness, and other therapeutic strategies. As we stand on the threshold of this chapter, we are about to embark on a journey in the profound transformative realm of spirituality.

In the face of trauma, we often find ourselves compelled to wear a facade of strength, concealing our inner turmoil. But true power lies in authenticity, in embracing the depths of our being and allowing spirituality to guide us to the path to resilience.

In the following pages, we will uncover the profound potential of spirituality to be a source of inner peace, strength, and renewed purpose. This chapter will introduce you to various spiritual practices, including meditation, prayer, and mindfulness techniques, which can enrich your soul and fuel your resilience. As we dive into the heart of this chapter, let us embrace the profound impact of spirituality in our journey toward healing. By tapping into our spiritual selves, we open ourselves to newfound strength and meaning, lighting the way forward to greater resilience and enduring growth.

A HEALING STORY

In the quiet town of Hopeville, nestled in the heart of the mountains, lived a woman named Emma. Her story would inspire the most skeptical minds to believe in the transformative power of spirituality. Emma had endured hardship that no one could fathom, carrying the weight of trauma that had clouded her life for many years. But she was determined to find solace, resilience, and healing through her spiritual journey. Emma's story of healing began with an ancestral legacy of trauma passed down through generations. Her family had endured struggles, conflicts, and unimaginable hardships. Growing up, she often found herself lost in a sea of confusion, grappling with the ghosts of the past. The scars ran deep, affecting every facet of her life, from her relationships to her sense of self.

One day, while Emma was visiting her grandmother, a wise and gentle woman who had weathered her own share of life's storms, something extraordinary happened. Her grandmother took her hand and led her to a secluded spot in the garden, a place where they had shared countless stories and quiet moments. As they sat together, her grandmother began to speak of the importance of spirituality. She shared stories of resilience, courage, and the indomitable human spirit. Emma listened with rapt attention, her heart swelling with the realization that there was a path toward healing that she had yet to explore.

Inspired by her grandmother's wisdom, Emma embarked on a journey of self-discovery and spiritual exploration. She began to attend mindfulness meditation classes at a local community center, where she learned the art of being present in the moment. Meditation allowed her to still the turbulence within her and connect with the depths of her soul. It was in these moments of silence and introspection that Emma found a newfound strength to confront her past.

In addition to meditation, Emma started small steps into the world of prayer. She sought solace in her spiritual community, drawing strength from their shared faith. The act of prayer became a lifeline, connecting her with a higher power that provided comfort and guidance. Emma's faith allowed her to release the burdens of her past and forgive those who had inflicted her wounds.

Emma's journey also led her to explore the healing power of nature. She spent hours hiking in the mountains, basking in the tranquility of the wilderness. With each step, she felt a renewed sense of connection with the universe. The rustling leaves, babbling brooks, and towering trees whispered words of solace, reminding her of the beauty that could be found even in the most tumultuous times.

With time, Emma's spiritual journey began to bear fruit. She discovered that spirituality was not about escaping her pain but finding the strength to face it head-on. Her resilience grew, and she realized that she could shape her destiny and transcend the cycle of intergenerational trauma. Emma's story serves as a testament to the transformative power of spirituality. She found her path to healing through mindfulness, prayer, and a deep connection with nature. Once buried beneath layers of trauma, her resilience shone through, illuminating her life with a profound sense of peace and purpose.

As we navigate the chapters of our lives, we often encounter adversity, but Emma's story reminds us that spirituality can be a guiding light in the darkest times. It teaches us that healing is possible, even from the deepest wounds, when we open our hearts to the transformative power of the spiritual journey.

Spirituality in Trauma Recovery

Trauma is a deeply personal experience, often leaving you with profound emotional scars that can be challenging to heal. The journey toward recovery is multifaceted, involving various therapeutic approaches, and spirituality plays a significant role in this process. It provides a unique avenue for us to find solace, inner strength, and meaning in the aftermath of trauma.

Trauma, whether resulting from physical, emotional, or psychological experiences, can profoundly affect an individual's spiritual well-being. It can shatter a person's sense of security, leading to despair, hopelessness, and spiritual questioning. This disruption in the spiritual domain is particularly prevalent in situations where the trauma challenges one's deeply held beliefs or sense of purpose.

Conversely, spirituality can significantly influence our response to trauma. It provides a framework for understanding suffering and finding meaning within it. For many, spirituality acts as a source of comfort, resilience, and coping mechanisms. It can instill a sense of hope and help you regain a sense of control over your life.

THE POSITIVE AND NEGATIVE INTERPLAY

The interplay between spirituality and trauma can yield both positive and negative outcomes. Positively, spirituality often offers a sense of transcendence, allowing us to connect with something greater than ourselves, which can lead to feelings of peace and serenity. The act of prayer, meditation, or engaging in spiritual rituals can promote relaxation and reduce the symptoms of stress that commonly accompany trauma. Moreover, spiritual communities can provide a support network for us to lean on during difficult times, reducing feelings of isolation.

However, it's essential to recognize the potential negative aspects of the relationship between spirituality and trauma. For some, trauma can lead to a spiritual crisis and profound questioning. Why did this happen? Why would a higher power allow such suffering? Such questions can challenge one's faith and contribute to feelings of anger, confusion, and despair. The intersection of spirituality and trauma is a deeply personal journey, and while many find solace in spirituality, others may find themselves questioning or even abandoning their spiritual beliefs.

THE ROLE OF SPIRITUALITY IN THE RECOVERY PROCESS

Spirituality can be a powerful and versatile tool in the trauma recovery process. It offers several valuable contributions to the healing journey, including:

- Trauma often disrupts our sense of meaning and purpose. Spirituality can provide a framework for making sense of the suffering, enabling us to find purpose and value in our experiences.

- Engaging in spiritual practices can foster resilience by encouraging us to draw upon our inner strength and maintain hope even in the face of adversity.
- Prayer, meditation, and other spiritual practices can serve as effective coping mechanisms to manage the overwhelming emotions and stress that trauma brings.
- Spiritual communities and networks provide a sense of belonging and emotional support that can alleviate feelings of isolation and loneliness that often accompany trauma.
- Spirituality can promote self-compassion, encouraging us to forgive ourselves and find inner peace.

Spirituality's relationship with trauma is multifaceted, with both positive and negative aspects. While it may not be a one-size-fits-all solution, it undoubtedly plays a significant role in the recovery process. It offers the potential to restore hope, inner peace, and a sense of purpose to all of us who have experienced trauma, contributing to our journey of healing and resilience.

Spiritual Approaches

Spirituality provides us with tools and practices to connect with a higher power, find solace, and cope with the emotional scars of our experiences. In the exploration of spiritual approaches to healing trauma, we look into the value of connecting with healing power and the power of prayer as essential components in the recovery process.

Connecting with a higher power is a cornerstone of many spiritual practices. This approach provides us with a profound sense of support, guidance, and purpose. For those dealing with trauma, connecting to a higher power can offer a source of solace and strength. Research conducted by The Mental Desk (Phillips, 2022) has shown that this connection can be a valuable component in trauma recovery.

A study conducted by the National Center for PTSD (*PTSD: National Center for PTSD*, n.d.) confirms that those who incorporate spiritual practices involving a higher power in their trauma recovery reported significant improvements in their mental health and overall well-being. The study found that those who developed a meaningful relationship with a higher power experienced reduced symptoms of anxiety and depression, as well as enhanced feelings of hope, inner peace, and resilience.

To connect with a higher power, you often engage in practices such as meditation, prayer, or involvement in a spiritual community. These practices can foster a sense of belonging and emotional support, which is especially crucial for those who have experienced trauma. When someone cultivates a sense of connection with a higher power, they often report a restored sense of purpose and an increased ability to make sense of their cultivated suffering.

One common misconception is that connecting with a higher power requires adherence to a specific religious doctrine. However, the process is deeply personal and adaptable to one's beliefs. It doesn't necessarily involve affiliating with a religious tradition; it can also manifest in developing a personal, spiritual connection with a force greater than oneself.

HOW TO CONNECT TO A HIGHER POWER

Connecting to a higher power is a profoundly personal and adaptable process that transcends specific religious affiliations. Here are some steps to help you establish and nurture this connection:

- Start by reflecting on your beliefs and values. What do you consider sacred or transcendent? What higher power of divine entity resonates with you? It could be a monotheistic God, a pantheon of deities, nature, the universe, or any other concept that holds personal significance.
- Explore different religious or spiritual traditions to find one that aligns with your beliefs and values. Attend services, read sacred texts, or engage with communities that share your perspective.

- Prayer and meditation are powerful tools to connect with a higher power. They provide a space for open and honest communication with the divine. Develop a regular practice of prayer or meditation to establish this connection.
- Engage in rituals or ceremonies that hold spiritual significance for you. Lighting candles, offering gratitude, or participating in sacred ceremonies can deepen your connection.
- Being mindful of the present moment and cultivating a sense of presence can enhance your connection to a higher power. Recognize the divine in the beauty of the natural world, the kindness of others, or the stillness within yourself.
- If you're uncertain about your beliefs or how to establish a connection, seek guidance from spiritual mentors, clergy, or counselors who can provide insights and support.
- Embrace compassion for yourself and others. Recognize that your connection to a higher power can foster a sense of love, empathy, and forgiveness.
- Engaging in acts of service and kindness can strengthen your connection to a higher power. By helping others, you can manifest the divine in your actions.
- Maintain a journal to record your thoughts, prayers, and experiences related to your connection with a

higher power. This can serve as a source of reflection and growth.

- Establishing a nurturing a connection to a higher power is a journey that unfolds over time. Trust the process and remain open to the signs, insights, and guidance that may come your way.

Connecting to a higher power can be a deeply transformative and healing experience, particularly in the context of trauma recovery. Whether you find solace in a traditional religious context or through a more personal and eclectic spiritual path, this connection has the potential to be a source of hope, healing, and resilience on your journey to recovery.

PRAYER

Prayer is a widely recognized and practiced spiritual approach you use to find solace, guidance, and healing, particularly in times of trauma. The power of prayer resides in its capacity to facilitate an open and honest dialogue with a higher power, enabling you to express your emotions, seek comfort, and find guidance. Prayer can lead to self-discovery and emotional healing by allowing you to release feelings of anger, resentment, or despair associated with tier traumatic experiences.

Prayer is a deeply personal practice that can be adapted to your beliefs, making it a powerful tool for trauma recovery.

It encourages a sincere connection with one's spiritual beliefs. Prayer does not have strict guidelines for trauma recovery, making it a personal and adaptable practice. To get started, create a space that encourages open dialogue with a higher power or one's spiritual beliefs. You can express your emotions, concerns, or struggles sincerely and openly. This practice can lead to emotional relief, self-compassion, and acceptance, which are crucial for healing.

For those who follow Christian or other religious traditions, specific prayer and Bible scriptures can provide comfort and strength during trauma recovery. These resources offer guidance, hope, and inspiration to navigate the challenges associated with traumatic experiences.

- **Healing Prayers:** These prayers are a powerful way to request inner healing and relief from the emotional scars of trauma. They provide a source of comfort and assurance that one is not alone in your suffering.
- **Bible Scriptures for Healing and Strength:** Many Bable verses offer solace and inspiration for those on the path to recovery. Verses like Psalm 34: 18, "*The Lord is close to the brokenhearted and saves those who are crushed in spirit*" (*King James Bible*, 2017/1760, Psalms 34:18), provide comfort and remind us that we are not alone on this journey.

Connecting with a higher power and the power of prayer are essential components of spiritual approaches to healing trauma. These practices profoundly benefit mental health, emotional healing, and overall well-being. Whether through personal connections or religious traditions, these approaches can be instrumental in the recovery process, helping you find solace, strength, and a sense of purpose in the face of trauma.

Energy Healing

Energy healing practices like Reiki are becoming increasingly recognized for their ability to aid in trauma recovery. Reiki, in particular, has shown promise in helping you cope with the emotional aftermath of traumatic experiences.

Reiki, known as energy healing, originated in Japan. The word *Reiki* is created from two Japanese words: "Rei," which means universal, and "Ki," meaning life energy. Practitioners of *Reiki* strongly believe that a universal life force (energy) that flows within us can be used and transferred from the practitioner to the patient and is all around us as a healing power (*The Power of Reiki in Healing Trauma*, n.d.). When the energy becomes disrupted or imbalanced, it can lead to physical or emotional distress. Reiki aims to realign and restore this energy balance, promoting healing and well-being.

THE POWER OF REIKI IN HEALING TRAUMA

- **Stress Reduction:** Trauma often results in heightened stress levels. Reiki has been found to reduce stress and promote relaxation, enabling trauma survivors to find respite from the constant vigilance and anxiety that often accompany trauma.
- **Emotional Release:** Reiki can help release pent-up emotions and trauma-related blockages. It offers a safe space to process your emotions, fostering emotional healing.
- **Energetic Balance:** Trauma can disrupt an individual's energetic balance. Reiki focuses on restoring balance, addressing not only the physical but also the emotional and spiritual aspects of a person.
- **Sense of connection**: Trauma can lead to feelings of isolation and disconnection. Reiki sessions provide a sense of connection to the Reiki practitioner and the universal life energy, creating a supportive and comforting environment.

Reiki sessions are typically conducted in a serene and calming environment. During a session, the practitioner places their hand slightly on or near the recipient's body. Energy flows from the practitioner to the recipient, promoting relaxation and a sense of well-being. It is important to understand that Reiki is not a replacement for traditional therapy or medical treatment. Instead, it can be a complementary practice that enhances the healing process for trauma survivors.

Coping with Shame

Shame and guilt are complex emotions that frequently accompany trauma experiences. These emotions can manifest in various ways, complicating the recovery journey. Let's delve into the role of shame and guilt in trauma and explore coping strategies for dealing with these challenging feelings.

Shame is often a pervasive feeling for trauma survivors. This emotion arises from a sense of being fundamentally flawed, unworthy, or inherently bad due to traumatic experiences. Whether it's the shame of being a victim or feelings of guilt about not preventing the trauma, these emotions can significantly impact an individual's self-esteem and self-worth. Shame can lead to a range of detrimental behaviors, such as withdrawal, self-isolation, and even self-destructive tendencies. Acknowledging and addressing shame is crucial for trauma recovery. Coping with shame involves:

- Practice self-compassion by acknowledging that shame is a common response to trauma. Treat yourself with the same kindness and understanding you would offer to a friend facing similar circumstances.
- Open up to a trusted friend, family member, or therapist about your feelings of shame. Sharing your

experiences with someone you trust can help alleviate this emotional burden.

- Identify and challenge negative thoughts that perpetuate feelings of shame. Replace these with more positive and compassionate self-talk.
- Consider trauma-focused therapy, which can help you explore the roots of your shame and work through these feelings in a safe and supportive environment.

COPING WITH GUILT

Guilt is another complex emotion that can emerge from trauma. It often takes the form of survivor guilt, where you feel responsible for surviving while others did not or for not preventing the traumatic event. Guilt can become a significant barrier to recovery and well-being. Coping with guilt involves:

- Recognize that survivors' guilt and other forms of guilt are common responses to trauma. This acknowledgment can be the first step in addressing these feelings.
- Practice self-forgiveness by understanding that you were not at fault for the traumatic event. Accepting this truth can help reduce guilt.
- Joining support groups or speaking with others who have experienced similar feelings of guilt can provide

validation and understanding.

- Incorporate mindfulness and meditation practices into your daily routine to foster self-awareness and alleviate guilt.

Soul-Restoring Affirmations

Affirmations are a powerful tool to use in healing from trauma. These are positive statements or phrases that you can use to shift your mindset, cultivate self-compassion, and restore your sense of self-worth after trauma. Here are 20 soul-restoring affirmation that caters to trauma recovery.

- I am safe and protected.
- I am stronger than my trauma.
- I release the past and embrace my present.
- I deserve healing and happiness.
- I am resilient, and I can overcome anything.
- I am worthy of love and support.
- I forgive myself and others.
- I trust the journey of my healing.
- I am not defined by my past.
- I am in control of my thoughts and emotions.
- I am grateful for each day's blessings.
- I can find peace within myself.
- I am worthy of self-compassion and self-care.
- I have the courage to face my trauma.
- I am healing and growing stronger every day.
- I let go of the pain, and I am free.

- I am capable of creating a bright future.
- I choose love and light over fear and darkness.
- I am a survivor, and I am resilient.
- I trust in my inner strength and wisdom.

In this chapter, we explored the profound connection between spirituality and trauma recovery. We witnessed how spirituality can offer strength, solace, and meaning to those who have experienced trauma. Whether through practices like Reiki, addressing complex emotions like shame and guilt, or harnessing the power of affirmations, you have various tools at your disposal to foster resilience and healing.

As we move forward into the next chapter, *In the Eye of the Storm: Facing Trauma Head On,* we will delve deeper into confronting trauma, understanding its impacts, and learning how to navigate the path to recovery. This journey may be challenging, but it leads toward growth, strength, and, ultimately, healing.

6

IN THE EYE OF THE STORM: FACING TRAUMA HEAD-ON

If you continue to carry bricks from your past, you will end up building the same house.

— UNKNOWN

As we start this chapter, we are reminded of the profound impact of our past experiences. Just like carrying bricks from the past, if we don't address the trauma we've endured, we risk bringing the same patterns and experiences into our future. This chapter is dedicated to confronting the storm and facing trauma head-on to build our lives with resilience and strength.

In the eye of the storm, we find a place of relative calm and clarity. Here, amid the chaos, we are presented with a choice: to either perpetuate the destructive cycles of trauma or break free from its grasp. Just as a storm can reshape the landscape, trauma can alter the course of our lives. This chapter guides us through the process of weathering storms, reshaping our path, and forging ahead with newfound determination.

Throughout this chapter, we will explore the intricate ways trauma affects our lives, minds, and relationships. We will discuss the importance of confronting our past, acknowledging our pain, and dealing with the emotions we've long held within. We will navigate the challenging terrain of trauma recovery, learning to process our experiences and find the strength to heal.

The following pages serve as a beacon of hope, illuminating the path toward recovery and transformation. As we confront the storm, we will gain a deeper understanding of ourselves, rediscover our resilience, and begin to rebuild our lives on a foundation of healing. Together, we'll walk through the pain, learn to let go of the bricks we've carried from the past, and find the power to construct a new, more resilient future.

WHY YOU SHOULD CONFRONT YOUR TRAUMA

In the depths of our being, we often carry the weight of unresolved experiences that haunt us, shape our reactions, and cast shadows over our lives. For some, the instinctual response is to deny or avoid these painful memories, believing that by doing so, they can be locked away, never to resurface. But the truth is that denying or avoiding trauma only perpetuates its hold on us. It is, therefore, essential to explore the profound reasons why confronting your trauma is the most powerful step towards healing.

- **Unleash the Shackles of the Past.** Trauma often serves as an anchor, keeping us tethered to the past. Confronting your trauma allows you to release these mental and emotional shackles, enabling you to break free from the relentless cycle of revisiting painful memories. As you confront your trauma, you create an opportunity for genuine healing and transformation. By facing your past, you gain the power to rewrite your future.
- **Reclaim Your Inner Peace.** Denying your trauma may offer momentary relief, but it rarely results in sustained inner peace. These buried memories can fester, leading to long-term emotional turmoil, stress, and even physical health issues. By confronting your trauma, you open the door to a profound sense of peace. As you address the pain,

you gradually free yourself from the weight that has burdened your soul.

- **Find Meaning and Empowerment.** Confronting your trauma can be empowering. It shifts the narrative from one of victimhood to one of survivorship. As you delve into the depths of your experiences, you have the opportunity to uncover meaning, strength, and resilience. This process can reshape your perspective, fostering personal growth and transformation.

- **Heal the Wounds that Fester.** Ignoring your trauma is like neglecting a festering wound. In the short term, it might seem tolerable, but the underlying infection continues to spread. Confronting your trauma, on the other hand, is akin to cleaning and dressing the wound. It may be painful but is a crucial step toward true healing.

- **Strengthen Relationships.** Untreated trauma can infiltrate your relationships, creating a cycle of pain that affects both you and those close to you. By confronting your trauma, you take a significant step towards mending these connections. When you heal yourself, you can engage in healthier, more fulfilling relationships with others.

While facing your trauma is essential for healing, it's important to acknowledge the nuanced role that trauma denial can play in the process. Trauma denial can offer short-term relief from overwhelming emotions, allowing you to maintain some semblance of daily functioning. This psychological defense mechanism can be viewed as a coping strategy that shields the psyche from the full impact of traumatic memories.

Although denial may provide a temporary escape from the pain, it can't offer a lasting solution. Trauma denial merely delays the inevitable confrontation with these experiences. The longer you postpone addressing your trauma, the more deeply it can become ingrained in your psyche. Trauma denial often leads to the repression of painful memories, locking them away in the deep recesses of the mind. However, these memories do not simply vanish; instead, they may resurface at unexpected moments, intensifying your emotional distress.

Denying your trauma can lead to strained relationships with loved ones who might not understand the root of your emotional struggles. It can create confusion, distance, and frustration within these connections.

In the tumultuous journey of healing from trauma, confronting your past experiences is a critical step on the path to recovery. By doing so, you unleash the shackles of the past, find inner peace, and uncover meaning and empowerment. Healing your wounds and strengthening relationships become possible as you bravely face your trauma.

Trauma denial, while offering temporary relief, is a double-edged sword. It can provide short-term respite from emotional distress, but it does not offer lasting solutions. Instead, it postpones the inevitable confrontation with your unresolved pain, which may ultimately resurface in more insidious ways.

What it Means to Process Your Trauma

Trauma leaves an indelible mark on our lives. It can warp our perceptions, affect our behavior, and cast long shadows on our mental and emotional well-being. To navigate the aftermath of trauma, one crucial step is to process these experiences. Trauma processing is the psychological and emotional work required to make sense of and ultimately heal from traumatic experiences. It involves acknowledging the pain, emotions, and memories associated with the trauma and integrating them into your narrative. The goal of processing is not to erase the past but to enable you to carry it differently, transforming the trauma from a shackle into a stepping stone.

Trauma processing is the psychological and emotional work required to make sense of and ultimately heal from traumatic experiences. It involves acknowledging the pain, emotions, and memories associated with the trauma and integrating them into your narrative. The goal of processing is not to erase the past but to enable you to carry it differently, transforming the trauma from a shackle into a stepping stone.

- **Acceptance and Acknowledgment:** One of the first steps in processing trauma is to accept that the traumatic event occurred. It requires acknowledgment that you were, in fact, a victim of a traumatic experience. This step can be emotionally challenging, forcing you to confront painful memories and emotions you may have been trying to avoid.

- **Emotional Expression and Catharsis:** Processing trauma entails allowing ourselves to feel and express the emotions associated with the traumatic event. This includes acknowledging anger, grief, sadness, and fear. Emotional catharsis can take many forms, such as talking about your feelings with a trusted friend or therapist, journaling, or engaging in creative activities that help you express your emotions.

- **Integration and Narrative Reconstruction:** Trauma processing also involves weaving the traumatic experience into your life story. It means finding a way to incorporate the trauma into your narrative without letting it define you. This step is crucial for reclaiming a sense of agency and control over your own life.

- **Healing and Growth:** Ultimately, processing your trauma should lead to healing and personal growth. It's about recognizing how the traumatic event has shaped your life and learning from it. Trauma can be a catalyst for self-discovery, fostering resilience and inner strength.

TIPS FOR TRAUMA PROCESSING

The journey of processing trauma may be daunting, but it is a crucial part of healing. Here are some essential tips to help you get started:

- Therapists, counselors, and mental health professionals are experts in guiding you through trauma processing. They can provide a safe and supportive environment for you to explore your traumatic experiences and emotions.
- Writing about your experiences, thoughts, and feelings can be a powerful way to process trauma. Journaling offers a structured and reflective process to help you make sense of your emotions and memories.
- Connect with support groups or online communities where you can share your experiences with people who have faced similar traumas. This sense of belonging can be profoundly comforting and validating.
- Engage in creative activities such as art, music, or dance to express your emotions. Creative outlets can help you process trauma in a nonverbal and deeply personal way.

- Mindfulness practices can help you stay present and cultivate self-compassion while processing your trauma. Meditation and deep breathing exercises can help you manage distressing emotions and thoughts.
- Remember that processing trauma is not a race. It is a gradual and nonlinear journey. Be patient with yourself and acknowledge that healing can take time.

Exposure Techniques

Facing and processing trauma can be an arduous journey, fraught with anxiety, distress, and fear. The experiences that haunt you demand resolution, and exposure techniques are valuable tools that help you confront and ultimately overcome your traumatic past. Let's dive right into the world of exposure techniques, exploring their significance, types, and applications in trauma processing. Each technique holds the promise of healing, allowing you to regain control of your life and emotions.

UNDERSTANDING EXPOSURE TECHNIQUES

Exposure techniques are a cornerstone of trauma processing therapies. They are designed to help you confront distressing memories, thoughts, and situations related to your traumatic experiences. By safely approaching these triggers and gradually desensitizing themselves, you can regain mastery over your emotional responses. The various exposure techniques are powerful tools for dismantling the grip trauma holds over one's life. Let's explore the nuances of each approach:

Imaginal Exposure

Imaginal exposure is a powerful technique often used to treat you with Post-Traumatic Stress Disorder (PTSD). It involves vividly imagining traumatic events or situations in detail. This technique can be particularly beneficial in addressing distressing, intrusive thoughts or traumatic memories. Here is the procedure:

- **Preparation and Rationale:** Before beginning imaginal exposure, a therapist will provide a thorough explanation of the process, outlining the rationale and expected benefits. You are encouraged to approach this technique with an open and inquisitive mindset.
- **Emotional Processing Preparation:** During this step, you explore your emotional readiness for the upcoming process. You learn about your emotional reactions and coping mechanisms, laying the foundation for effective processing.
- **Imaginal Exposure:** In this pivotal stage, you recount the traumatic event verbally or in writing. This process allows them to engage with your narrative, revisiting the details of the trauma. It may be emotionally challenging, but it is essential for healing.

- **Integration:** After imaginal exposure, you work with your therapists to process the emotions and thoughts that emerge during the exercise. Integration involves discussing any new insights and reinforcing a sense of safety and control.

In-Vivo Exposure

In-vivo exposure is a highly effective therapeutic technique, particularly beneficial for those struggling with specific phobias, anxiety disorders, and PTSD. It involves confronting real-life situations, triggers, or environments associated with distress and fear. By gradually and systematically exposing you to these situations, in-vivo exposure aims to reduce your emotional reactions, anxiety, and avoidance behavior. Let's delve into a more detailed understanding of in-vivo exposure, including its procedure and importance.

Exposure techniques are a vital component of trauma processing. These techniques enable you to approach rather than avoid memories and situations related to the traumatic event. By doing so, you gain control over your reactions and diminish the power that the trauma has over your life. Here are some exposure techniques to consider:

- **Gradual Exposure**: Gradual exposure involves facing trauma-related memories or situations incrementally. It allows you to build tolerance and resilience over time. A therapist or counselor can guide you in designing an exposure plan that suits your pace and comfort level.

- **Narrative Exposure:** Narrative exposure encourages you to share your traumatic experiences in detail. You might recount your story verbally or in writing. By engaging with your narrative, you gradually desensitize the distress associated with the trauma.

- **Virtual Reality Exposure Therapy (VRET)**: VRET is an innovative approach that uses virtual reality to recreate and confront trauma-related environments or situations in a controlled and safe setting. It allows you to confront your trauma while maintaining a sense of safety.

- **Imaginal Exposure**: Imaginal exposure involves vividly imagining traumatic events or situations in a safe and controlled environment. This approach is often combined with cognitive-behavioral techniques to help modify distorted beliefs about the trauma.

- **Sensory Exposure:** Sensory exposure aims to address trauma through the senses. It might involve touching objects or engaging in sensory activities that connect with the traumatic experience. By using the senses, you can process emotions and memories more effectively.

The Procedure of In-Vivo Exposure Includes:

- **Assessment and Hierarchy Development:** The process begins with a comprehensive assessment conducted by a mental health professional, during which your specific fears and triggers are identified. To implement in-vivo exposure effectively, it's crucial to create an exposure hierarchy, which is a structured list of situations or scenarios related to your trauma or phobia. This list is organized from the least distressing to the most distressing, ensuring a gradual progression.

- **Education and Preparation:** Before embarking on in-vivo exposure, the therapist educates you about the rationale behind the technique and its structure. Then you learn that the purpose is not to overwhelm but to provide a systematic and controlled way to confront your fears.

- **Exposure:** You begin by confronting situations at the lower end of your exposure hierarchy. For example, someone with a phobia of heights might start by standing near a low ledge in a secure environment. The therapist accompanies you, providing support and guidance.

- **Response Prevention:** You are discouraged from using avoidance behavior or safety-seeking tactics during exposure. They are encouraged to experience the anxiety or distress associated with the situation fully. For instance, if someone with social anxiety is practicing in-vivo exposure by attending a social event, they would be discouraged from leaving early or excessively using their phone as a coping mechanism.

- **Progressive Exposure:** Over time, you systematically work your way up the exposure hierarchy, moving toward more distressing situations. The goal is to experience each situation long enough for the anxiety or distress to reduce significantly. The progression is based on Your readiness and comfort level.
- **Regular Practice:** In-vivo exposure is often a consistent part of your therapy sessions, with each session dedicated to confronting different situations from the exposure hierarchy. Regular practice is essential to achieving progress.
- **Discussion and Reflection:** After each exposure exercise, you engage in discussions with their therapists about your experiences. you share your thoughts, emotions, and physical sensations, which help process the exposure's impact.

In-vivo exposure is a cornerstone of trauma and anxiety therapy due to its effectiveness in reducing distressing emotional reactions and avoidance behaviors. The technique helps you regain control over your life by gradually dismantling the fear associated with traumatic triggers.

The exposure hierarchy ensures that you have a structured path to follow, which is critical in preventing overwhelming exposure scenarios. By gradually exposing yourself to distressing situations, you build tolerance, confidence, and a sense of empowerment. As you conquer each situation on your hierarchy, your fear and avoidance decrease, ultimately leading to a significant reduction in your overall emotional distress.

Interoceptive Exposure

Interoceptive exposure is a specialized therapeutic technique often used in the treatment of anxiety disorders, including post-traumatic stress disorder (PTSD). It is designed to help you confront and desensitize yourself to the physical sensations associated with anxiety. Here's a comprehensive look at the procedure and significance of interoceptive exposure:

- **Understanding Physical Sensations:** The initial step in interoceptive exposure is psychoeducation. You are educated about the physiological sensations that are often associated with anxiety. These sensations may include an increased heart rate, shortness of breath, dizziness, muscle tension, stomach discomfort, and other bodily responses. You are made aware that these physical sensations are natural bodily reactions to anxiety and are not inherently harmful.

- **Exposure Exercises:** The core of interoceptive exposure involves a series of structured exercises intentionally designed to provoke specific physical sensations related to anxiety. These exercises are carried out in a controlled and monitored environment with the guidance of a mental health professional. They are tailored to induce particular physical responses. For example, controlled hyperventilation may be used to induce dizziness, and breath-holding exercises might trigger a sense of suffocation. The aim is not to harm but to provoke specific responses.

- **Desensitization:** Over time, as you repeatedly engage in these exposure exercises, you become more accustomed to the discomfort associated with these physical sensations. The systematic desensitization process helps break the connection between these sensations and the distressing emotions linked to them. The goal is for you to develop tolerance and reduce their anxiety response. Through these exercises, you learn that the physical sensations of anxiety are not inherently dangerous and that they can be managed.

Significance of Interoceptive Exposure

Interoceptive exposure is a vital technique in treating anxiety disorders and related conditions, as it addresses the fear of anxiety itself rather than specific external triggers. Its significance can be summarized as follows:

- **Emotional Processing**. Interoceptive exposure allows you to engage in emotional processing by confronting the very core of your anxiety-the fear of anxiety itself. This process helps you recognize that your emotional distress is often tied to your physical sensations. This understanding is a significant step towards healing.

- **Reduce Avoidance.** Many individuals with anxiety disorders, including PTSD, tend to avoid situations that may provoke anxiety-related physical sensations. Interoceptive exposure encourages you to face and manage these sensations, thereby reducing your inclination to avoid certain situations. This can lead to a broader, more fulfilling life as you learn to cope effectively with various stressors.

- **Enhanced Coping Skills.** Those who have undergone interoceptive exposure often report improved coping skills. They develop a deeper understanding of their physical responses to anxiety and learn how to manage these reactions more effectively. As a result, they experience better stress management and overall emotional resilience.

- **Reduced Anxiety Sensitivity.** Anxiety sensitivity refers to the fear of experiencing anxiety-related symptoms. Interoceptive exposure directly targets this fear, helping you overcome your anxiety sensitivity. You often experience less fear and distress during anxious moments, as they have learned to manage and confront anxiety-related physical sensations.

PROLONGED EXPOSURE AND PROCEDURE

Prolonged exposure is a widely used and highly effective therapeutic technique specifically designed for the treatment of PTSD. This approach encourages you to systematically confront trauma-related memories, triggers, and thoughts. By repeatedly and gradually approaching these distressing elements, you can reduce your emotional reactions and regain control over your lives. Here is the procedure:

- **Education and Preparation:** The process begins with educating you about the rationale and structure of prolonged exposure therapy. You are informed that confronting your traumatic memories is a pivotal step toward healing. You learn about the purpose of the therapy and understand that it involves revisiting and processing distressing memories.
- **Imaginal Exposure:** You are guided to engage in imaginal exposure, which entails recounting traumatic events either verbally or in writing. This phase encourages you to confront and process the

details of your trauma narrative, helping you face the emotional impact of your experiences. It is an essential part of desensitizing you to your traumatic memories.

- **In-Vivo Exposure:** In this phase, you confront real-life situations and triggers associated with your trauma. These situations are systematically approached through an exposure hierarchy, starting with less distressing triggers and progressing to more challenging ones. This gradual process is vital in reducing the emotional distress linked to these situations. You are encouraged to engage with trauma-related triggers as a way to regain control of your life.

- **Processing and Integration:** Following the exposure exercises, you work closely with their therapists to process the emotions and thoughts that emerge. This phase involves discussing new insights, challenges, and revelations brought about by the exposure exercises. The therapist helps you integrate your trauma experiences into their narratives. It allows you to make sense of your trauma, helping to reduce the emotional impact it has on your life.

Significance of Prolonged Exposure

Prolonged exposure therapy is a gold standard treatment for those dealing with PTSD. Its significance can be understood as follows:

- Prolonged exposure encourages you to confront your trauma head-on. By systematically addressing your traumatic memories, triggers, and thoughts, you regain control over your emotional responses. This confrontation helps you process your trauma and reduce the power it holds over your life.
- The therapy promotes desensitization by gradually exposing you to your trauma-related triggers. As you repeatedly face these distressing elements, your emotional reactions decrease. Over time, this reduces the distressing emotions associated with traumatic memories and triggers.
- Prolonged exposure therapy aids you in integrating your trauma experiences into your personal narratives. Through processing and discussion with your therapists, you make sense of your trauma, reducing its emotional impact. It allows you to move forward with your life, no longer held by your traumatic past.

Interoceptive exposure and prolonged exposure are two valuable therapeutic techniques that play a pivotal role in the treatment of anxiety disorders, PTSD, and trauma-related conditions. Interoceptive exposure helps you confront and desensitize yourself to anxiety-related physical sensations, leading to emotional processing, reduced avoidance, enhanced coping skills, and decreased anxiety sensitivity. Prolonged exposure therapy enables you to confront your trauma by systematically approaching your traumatic memories and triggers. This confrontation, along with desensitization and integration, helps you regain control over your emotional responses and move toward healing and recovery. When administered by skilled mental health professionals, these techniques empower you to process your trauma and anxiety, ultimately freeing yourself from the grip of your past traumas.

Exposure Therapies

Exposure therapies are a set of evidence-based therapeutic techniques that have proven highly effective in the treatment of various mental health conditions, including trauma-related disorders. The focus is on helping you confront and process distressing thoughts, memories, and emotions in a controlled and supportive environment. In this comprehensive exploration, we will delve into exposure therapies, specifically Cognitive Processing Therapy (CPT), Trauma-Focused Cognitive Behavioral Therapy (TF-CBT), Exposure and Response Prevention (ERP), and Narrative Exposure Therapy (NET). For each of these therapies, we will discuss how they work, when they are typically used, what to expect during treatment, and what to look for in a therapist.

COGNITIVE PROCESSING THERAPY (CPT)

- **How it Works:** CPT is a structured cognitive-behavioral treatment that aims to help you process traumatic experiences and related emotions by challenging and reframing maladaptive thoughts and beliefs. It is based on the premise that trauma can lead to distorted beliefs, such as self-blame or feelings of permanent vulnerability. CPT targets these beliefs through cognitive restructuring.

- **When It's Used:** CPT is a therapy often used to treat individuals suffering from post-traumatic stress disorder (PTSD) (Davis, 2020). PTSD can stem from a range of traumatic experiences in our lives, or it can stem from childhood trauma or neglect. CBT therapy is especially effective for addressing the cognitive aspects of trauma, helping individuals to break their experiences of trauma or belief systems we find challenging into smaller sections, and dealing with them in a positive manner.

- **What to Expect:** In CPT, you typically meet with a therapist once a week for approximately twelve sessions. Sessions are structured, and you are expected to complete homework assignments. Treatment involves psychoeducation, writing about the traumatic event in detail (a process known as the "trauma account"), identifying cognitive distortions, and challenging and reframing distorted beliefs through written exercises. The therapist guides and supports you throughout the process.

- **What to Look for in a Therapist:** A qualified CPT therapist should be trained in cognitive-behavioral therapy techniques, specifically CPT. Look for a licensed mental health professional, such as a psychologist or clinical social worker, with experience in treating trauma-related disorders.

TRAUMA-FOCUSED COGNITIVE BEHAVIORAL THERAPY (TF-CBT)

- **How it Works:** TF-CBT is a well-established approach that combines cognitive-behavioral techniques with trauma-focused interventions. It is designed to help you, especially children and adolescents, process your traumatic experiences, manage emotions, and develop healthy coping strategies.
- **When it's Used:** TF-CBT is primarily used for children and adolescents who have experienced trauma. It is effective for treating PTSD, as well as other emotional and behavioral issues that may arise as a result of trauma.
- **What to Expect:** TF-CBT typically involves 12-16 weekly sessions. Treatment components include psychoeducation, relaxation techniques, trauma narration and processing, cognitive coping, and in

vivo gradual exposure to trauma reminders. Both the child and their caregiver are actively involved in the therapy process.

- **What to Look for in a Therapist:** A TF-CBT therapist should have specialized training in this approach and experience working with children and adolescents. Licensed therapists, such as clinical psychologists or licensed clinical social workers, who have received TF-CBT certification are best suited for this therapy.

EXPOSURE AND RESPONSE PREVENTION (ERP)

- **How it Works:** ERP is a therapeutic technique primarily used to treat obsessive-compulsive disorder (OCD). It involves exposing you to your specific fears or obsessions while preventing the compulsive behaviors that typically follow to reduce anxiety. ERP helps you learn that they can tolerate anxiety without resorting to rituals or avoidance.
- **When It's Used:** ERP is used in the treatment of OCD and related disorders where compulsive behaviors and avoidance mechanisms are present.
- **What to Expect:** ERP therapy is structured and tailored to your specific OCD symptoms. Sessions usually involve exposing you to situations or thoughts that trigger your obsessions. The therapist helps you confront your fears and gradually reduce

the associated distress. Over time, anxiety diminishes as you learn that compulsions are not necessary for anxiety reduction.

- **What to Look for in a Therapist:** When seeking an ERP therapist, look for professionals with experience in treating OCD and specialized training in ERP. This may include licensed psychologists, psychiatrists, or social workers.

NARRATIVE EXPOSURE THERAPY (NET)

- **How it Works:** NET is a structured short-term treatment designed to address complex trauma, such as experiences of war, violence, or multiple traumatic events. NET focuses on helping you construct a coherent narrative of your life, integrating traumatic memories with your overall life story.
- **When it's Used:** NET is used to treat refugees and survivors of war or violence who have experienced prolonged and complex trauma. It is especially beneficial for those who struggle with post-traumatic stress symptoms.
- **What to Expect:** NET involves creating a chronological narrative of your life, including traumatic experiences. The therapist helps you process your traumatic memories within the context of your life story. The treatment typically consists of

8-12 sessions, with each session lasting 90-120 minutes.

- **What to Look for in a Therapist:** A therapist using NET should have training and experience in narrative therapy and knowledge of trauma treatment. Psychologists, clinical social workers, or counselors with experience in working with survivors of complex trauma are well-suited for NET.

Tips on Storytelling

Storytelling is an essential element in narrative exposure therapy and can enhance various forms of therapy. Here are some tips on effective storytelling:

- **Establish Trust.** Building a trusting therapeutic relationship is crucial for successful storytelling. You should feel safe and supported in sharing your stories.
- **Create a Timeline.** Help you create a chronological timeline of your life experiences, including traumatic events. This timeline will serve as the foundation for the narrative.
- **Encourage Emotion Expression.** You should be encouraged to express your emotions while sharing your stories. Emotional expression is a fundamental aspect of processing trauma.

- **Reframe and Integrate.** Throughout the storytelling process, the therapist should assist you in reframing your narrative, allowing them to integrate the traumatic experiences into your broader life story.
- **Gradual Exposure.** In some exposure therapies, storytelling may involve gradual exposure to traumatic memories or themes. The therapist should guide you through this process, ensuring it is done at a pace that is comfortable for you.

Exposure therapies like CPT, TF-CBT, ERP, and NEP have demonstrated effectiveness in helping you process trauma and related disorders. Each therapy is tailored to specific conditions and age groups, and they all require a skilled and trained therapist for successful implementation. These therapies offer hope and healing to those who have experienced trauma, guiding them toward recovery and a brighter future.

Creating Your Narrative

The process of creating your narrative is an exercise that allows you to construct a coherent life story that integrates your traumatic experiences into the larger context of your life. It is a vital step on the road to post-traumatic growth as it enables you to make sense of your past, understand the impact of trauma, and see how it has shaped who you are today.

Follow these easy instructions for creating your narrative:

- Choose a quiet and comfortable place where you can focus without distractions. You may want to have a journal or a computer available to write your thoughts.
- Create a timeline that outlines significant events in your life. This should include not only traumatic experiences but also positive moments, achievements, and personal milestones. Your life is a journey, and it's important to acknowledge all aspects of it.
- As you reach the point on your timeline where traumatic experiences occurred, take time to reflect. Write down the details of these events, your emotions, and your reactions at the time. Allow yourself to express your feelings openly.
- Explore the impact of these traumatic experiences on your life. Consider how they may have influenced your beliefs, behaviors, and relationships. Take note of both the negative and positive changes that have occurred as a result.
- Search for meaning in your experiences. What lessons have you learned from your trauma? How have these experiences shaped your values, priorities, or sense of purpose? Consider the strengths and coping mechanisms you've developed along the way.

- The next step is to integrate your trauma into your larger life narrative. Recognize that it is a part of your story but not the entirety of it. How have you, as an individual, evolved and grown as a result of these experiences?
- Celebrate your resilience and strength in navigating these challenges. It's essential to recognize the ways you've coped and the support you received from others.
- Creating your narrative can be a profound and emotional experience. If you find it overwhelming or need assistance, consider seeking the guidance of a mental health professional or therapist.
- As you create your narrative, remember that the journey to post-traumatic growth is an ongoing process. Embrace the changes and growth you've experienced, and continue to nurture your renewal.

The "Create your Narrative" exercise is a powerful tool for those seeking to understand and process their trauma. It is an essential step on the road to post-traumatic growth, as it allows you to acknowledge the past, find meaning, and transform your experiences into a source of strength and wisdom.

In the next chapter, "The Road to Post-Traumatic Growth and Personal Renewal," we will delve into the principles and strategies that can guide you on this transformative journey.

This chapter is dedicated to exploring the potential for growth and renewal that lies within the heart of every trauma survivor.

7

THE ROAD TO POST-TRAUMATIC GROWTH & PERSONAL RENEWAL

Instead of saying, 'I'm damaged, I'm broken, I have trust issues.' 'I say, 'I'm healing, I'm rediscovering myself, I'm starting over.

— HORACIO JONES

Trauma has the power to reshape our lives, leaving us with the scars of our experiences and the choices to define ourselves either by our wounds or our healing. The path to recovery is arduous and filled with obstacles, but it is a path that can lead to a life enriched with newfound strength, wisdom, and hope. In this last chapter, we explore the possibilities that lie beyond trauma, the potential for growth, and the capacity for renewal. It's a journey from victim to survivor and, ultimately, to a thriving, resilient individual. So, let's embark on this voyage of personal transformation and uncover how you can build a stronger, more resilient self from the ashes of trauma.

THE PHOENIX RISING FROM THE ASHES

Maggie's life was like a tranquil stream winding through a peaceful meadow until it took an unexpected turn. A traumatic event left her battered and broken, her life in tatters. She could have succumbed to the despair that involved her, but instead, she chose to rise like a phoenix from the ashes of her suffering.

Over time, Maggie began to rebuild her life, piece by piece. She found solace in art, expressing her inner turmoil through colors and brushstrokes. Her creativity became her sanctuary, where she could confront her trauma and weave it into something beautiful.

Maggie's story, as seen in The Guardian (Allardice, 2021), is a testament to the power of post-traumatic growth. It reminds us that no matter how dark the clouds of trauma may be, they can also bear the silver lining of renewal. Through resilience, self-discovery, and the choice to thrive, Maggie found something profoundly good in her life after the storm.

Trauma may wound us deeply, but it doesn't have to be the end of our story. Just as the phoenix emerges from the ashes, we, too, can rise, rebuild, and discover the strength and beauty within ourselves.

WHAT IS POST-TRAUMATIC GROWTH

The human spirit's resilience is a force to be reckoned with, even in the face of distress and trauma. After enduring the darkest storms, we often find ourselves not only surviving but thriving in the aftermath of trauma or distress. This phenomenon is known as Post-Traumatic Growth (PTG). This captivating journey transforms you in the wake of adversity, enabling you to understand your behavior, reaction, and self with positive results. Let's explore the concept of PTG, the theory behind it, and how you can navigate its various domains, elements, and signs. By the end of this exploration, you'll be equipped with the knowledge and tools needed to thrive beyond trauma.

The seeds of PTG are sown in the most challenging and traumatic moments of our lives. It's a process of profound personal transformation that occurs in the wake of adversity, creating an opportunity for positive change. While it's easy to equate trauma solely with suffering and distress, PTG reveals a different facet of the human experience. Trauma can catalyze growth, allowing you to develop new perspectives, deeper meanings, and a greater appreciation for life. As explained by Psych Central (*Post-Traumatic Growth*, n.d.), PTG represents the positive changes experienced by someone who survived a traumatic event.

PTG is not a random occurrence but a structured and organized process. It's based on a theory that helps us understand the transformative journey you go through following trauma. This theory explores how suffering can lead to growth and positive changes, demonstrating that our experiences, no matter how harrowing, can shape our character and provide invaluable life lessons.

UNPACKING THE FIVE DOMAINS OF GROWTH

To comprehend the scope of PTG, it's essential to explore the five key domains of growth:

- **Relating to Others:** Trauma often fosters a deeper connection with loved ones. It amplifies empathy, allowing you to offer meaningful support and strengthening your relationships.
- **Personal Strength:** Adversity can be a crucible for personal resilience and strength. It encourages you to cultivate inner fortitude and the belief in your capacity to overcome challenges.
- **New Possibilities:** After trauma, the world may look different, but it can also seem more abundant with possibilities. When you experience PTG, you could develop a heightened sense of purpose and a greater willingness to explore opportunities.
- **Appreciation of Life:** Surviving trauma can lead to a heightened awareness of the beauty and preciousness

of life. It fosters gratitude for simple moments and a profound understanding of life's impermanence.

- **Spiritual or Existential Change:** You may question your beliefs and values after trauma. This process can lead to profound spiritual or existential growth, helping you find meaning and purpose in new or rediscovered ways of being authentically you.

Understanding these domains provides a roadmap for your journey toward post-traumatic growth. By recognizing these areas and their potential for development, you can navigate your transformation more effectively.

Elements of Growth

PTG is not a single event but a collection of moments, experiences, and changes that collectively constitute personal growth. The Harvard Business Review (Tedeschi, 2020) outlines several key elements of growth that often emerge in the aftermath of trauma:

- **An Altered Sense of Self:** Trauma can profoundly change how you perceive yourself. It may lead to greater self-acceptance, self-compassion, and a redefined self-identity.
- **Revised Life Priorities:** Trauma often compels you to reevaluate your life goals and values. This can lead to a reordering of priorities, with a greater understanding of what truly matters.

- **Enhanced Resilience:** Surviving trauma builds resilience, the capacity to bounce back from adversity. This newfound strength allows you to cope more effectively with future challenges.
- **Improved Relationships:** Navigating trauma often deepens interpersonal relationships. It can lead to better communication, empathy, and emotional intimacy with loved ones.
- **Heightened Appreciation for Life:** Trauma survivors frequently develop a deeper sense of gratitude for life's simple pleasures, as well as a heightened awareness of the present moment. This appreciation enriches life quality.

SIGNS OF POST-TRAUMATIC GROWTH

As you embark on the journey of PTG, it's essential to recognize the signs of growth along the way. These signs can help you gauge your progress and appreciate the transformation unfolding within you:

- You may notice a greater emotional connection with others, fostering more meaningful and intimate relationships.
- The ability to cope with adversity and bounce back from setbacks becomes more pronounced.
- An elevated sense of gratitude for life and its many facets often emerges.

- A more profound understanding of who you are, coupled with a heightened sense of self-compassion and acceptance.
- A newfound or clarified sense of purpose and direction in life can surface, guiding your decisions and goals.
- You may find your capacity for empathy, compassion, and understanding deepens, enhancing your relationships.
- A willingness to explore new possibilities, try different experiences, and continually learn and evolve.

With these signs as your guidepost, you can journey through the challenges of PTG with greater clarity and direction.

Post-traumatic growth offers a beacon of hope in the aftermath of trauma. While the pain of adversity is real, it can also be a gateway to profound personal transformation. By understanding the theory, domains, elements, and signs of PTG, you can embrace the journey of growth and come to recognize the resilience, wisdom, and beauty that can arise from the ashes of trauma.

Why Trauma Is So Difficult to Bounce Back From

Recovering from trauma is a formidable challenge, a journey through emotional and psychological turmoil. It's a road with numerous obstacles, and at times, it may seem like an insurmountable climb. To grasp why trauma can be so challenging to overcome, we must delve into the depths of the complexities.

The journey of trauma recovery is akin to navigating a labyrinth, each turn and twist revealing new challenges. To understand the difficulties associated with trauma recovery, we can refer to Carolyn Spring's insightful analysis (Spring, n.d.). She highlights three key challenges that make trauma recovery an arduous endeavor:

- **Disconnection from the Self:** One of the fundamental challenges of trauma recovery is the disconnection that trauma imposes between you and your core self. Trauma disrupts your connection with your own identity, feelings, and experiences. It creates a gulf, often leading to feelings of emptiness and dissociation. This disconnection complicates the journey to recovery, as you must bridge the gap and reintegrate with your authentic self. This process of reconnection can be painful and disorienting but is essential for healing.
- **Toxic Shame:** Trauma is often accompanied by deep-seated shame. If you have experienced trauma, you may carry feelings of guilt, self-blame, and worthlessness. This shame can be profoundly debilitating, hindering the healing process. Confronting and resolving these feelings is a difficult and often painful task, as it requires a journey through the depths of self-worth and self-

compassion. Toxic shame reinforces the trauma's emotional grip, making it difficult to let go and move forward.

- **Fragmentation of Self:** Trauma has the power to fragment your sense of self. It shatters the cohesive sense of identity, causing you to compartmentalize your experiences and emotions. These fragments may contain elements of the traumatic event or painful emotions, making it challenging to reconcile and reintegrate these broken parts. Recovery often involves recognizing, accepting, and integrating these fragmented aspects, which can be a daunting task.

Trauma is not just an event that happens and ends; it's a weight that survivors often carry with them long after the event has occurred. It taints one's worldview, relationships, and self-perception. The healing journey is burdened by these complexities, demanding unwavering courage, patience, and self-compassion.

HOW TO ACHIEVE POST-TRAUMATIC GROWTH

Overcoming trauma and achieving post-traumatic growth necessitates more than mere resilience; it requires introspection and self-reflection. Self-reflection serves as a guiding compass on the path to recovery, helping you gain a deeper understanding of your beliefs, experiences, and emotions.

Self-reflection is a powerful tool that fosters growth, intro-spection, and personal development. It is the practice of examining one's thoughts, emotions, and experiences. In the context of trauma recovery and post-traumatic growth, self-reflection plays a pivotal role in recognizing and addressing the intricate facets of trauma.

- Self-reflection helps you gain clarity about your beliefs, perceptions, and reactions. It unveils the underlying factors that may be contributing to your trauma's impact on your life.
- Trauma can create patterns of behavior and thought. Self-reflection enables you to identify these patterns, shedding light on unhealthy coping mechanisms and cognitive distortions that may be hindering your progress.
- It encourages self-compassion and self-kindness. The journey to post-traumatic growth can be tumultuous; self-reflection reminds you to treat yourself with gentleness and empathy.
- It can serve as a means of healing and a bridge to understanding your trauma's impact on your life. By confronting your experiences through self-reflection, you can initiate the process of acceptance and transformation.

WAYS TO ENGAGE IN SELF-REFLECTION

Self-reflection can take various forms, and it's important to find the approach that resonates with you. The following are strategies to encourage self-reflection:

- **Journaling:** Keeping a journal is a potent way to reflect on your thoughts, emotions, and experiences. You can write freely about your trauma and its effects, allowing your innermost feelings to flow onto the pages.
- **Meditation and Mindfulness:** Mindfulness practices help you stay present and reflect on your inner state. Mindful breathing and meditation are powerful tools to explore your thoughts and emotions.
- **Dialogue**: Engaging in conversations with a trusted friend, family member, or therapist can facilitate self-reflection. Discussing our feelings and experiences with someone you trust can offer valuable insights and emotional support.
- **Creative Expression:** Art, music, and other forms of creative expression provide unique outlets for self-reflection. Creating art, writing poetry, or composing music can help you convey and explore your emotions.
- **Questioning Your Beliefs**: A more structured approach is self-reflection involves asking yourself

188 | SOPHIA L. RAY

specific questions. The questions may vary depending on your experiences and goals, but they typically prompt deeper introspections.

QUESTIONS TO ASK YOURSELF IN SELF-REFLECTION

Self-reflection can be an open-ended process, but asking specific questions can guide your introspection more effectively. Here are some questions to consider during your self-reflection journey:

- What are my core beliefs about myself and the world?
- How have my traumatic experiences influenced my self-image and self-worth?
- What coping mechanisms have I developed, and are they helping or hindering my growth?
- What recurring thoughts and emotions do I experience related to my trauma?
- What strengths and personal resources can I tap into for post-traumatic growth?

Self-reflection is a powerful catalyst for understanding and navigating the complexities of trauma recovery. By embarking on this journey of introspection, you open the door to personal growth and post-traumatic growth. While the path may be challenging, the rewards of healing and transformation are immeasurable.

Finding Meaning and Purpose in Life After Trauma

Trauma has the power to shatter lives, leaving you grappling with the aftermath of devastation and distress. It can strip away a sense of purpose, leaving you adrift in a sea of pain and confusion. However, amidst the ruins, the human spirit possesses an incredible ability to rebuild, and part of this reconstruction process involves finding meaning and purpose in life once more.

Recovery from trauma is not about alleviating distressing symptoms or moving beyond the pain. It's a profound transformation that involves creating a new narrative for one's life. This narrative is rooted in the meaning and purpose that you can derive from your experiences. The journey to meaning-making after trauma encompasses the following important aspects:

- **Acknowledging the Pain:** One of the initial steps in finding meaning after trauma is acknowledging the pain and suffering. It's essential to confront the reality of the traumatic event and the emotional upheaval it has caused.
- **Integrating the Experience:** Traumatic experiences often disrupt your existing understanding of the world. To make meaning, you must integrate these

experiences into your life story, reconciling them with pre-existing beliefs.

- **Reconstructing the Narrative:** Creating meaning involves reconstructing one's life narrative. This means examining the impact of the trauma on your identity, values, and life goals.
- **Connecting with Values:** Meaning often arises from alignment with one's core values. This may involve exploring and deepening one's values or clarifying what is truly important in life.
- **Resilience and Growth:** Meaning-making is not merely about adapting to the trauma but also recognizing the potential for personal growth and resilience that can emerge from the experiences

Several psychological models and frameworks can help you make sense of your experiences and find meaning in them. These models provide valuable insights into the process of meaning-making and the ways people navigate their journey toward recovery. One of these models, proposed by Margaret Stroebe and Henk Schut, is mentioned in the article *The Dual Process Model of Grief in Simple Terms,* (Applebury, 2021). This model describes a process of oscillation between loss-orientation and restoration-orientation. Loss-orientation focuses on grieving and traumatic events and processing the associated emotions, while restoration-orientation pertains to the pursuit of a new, meaningful life. This model underscores the importance of allowing individuals to go back and forth between these orientations as part of their meaning-making journey.

THE THREE-COMPONENT MODEL OF POST-TRAUMATIC GROWTH

This model, developed by psychologists Richard Tedeschi and Lawrence Calhoun, as mentioned in their research (Tedeschi, 2020d), highlights the potential for personal growth after trauma. It identifies three key components:

- **Cognitive:** Cognitive restructuring involves challenging and modifying negative thought patterns associated with the trauma. This may involve reappraising the event's significance and its impact on one's life.
- **Emotional:** Emotional processing is essential for making meaning. It entails confronting the emotions associated with the trauma, such as grief, anger, guilt, and fear. Processing these emotions can be painful but is crucial for healing.
- **Behavioral:** Behavioral changes may be necessary to align with one's newfound values and purpose. This may involve making significant life changes, pursuing new goals, or engaging in activities that promote well-being and a sense of purpose.

SOCIAL SUPPORT, RESILIENCE, AND MEANING-MAKING

Social support is a crucial factor in the meaning-making process. Interactions with friends, family, or support groups can provide individuals with a sense of belonging and validation. These relationships offer opportunities for you to share your experiences, gain perspective, and receive encouragement in your meaning-making journey.

Resilience plays a pivotal role in meaning-making after trauma. With resilience, you will demonstrate greater adaptability and find it easier to derive meaning from your experiences. By developing resilience, you can more effectively navigate the complexities of trauma recovery. Cultivating meaning and purpose after trauma is a deeply personal journey, but some strategies can aid in the process:

- **Seek Professional Help**. Therapists and counselors trained in trauma recovery can provide guidance and support in your meaning-making journey.
- **Connect with Support Groups**. Engaging with others who have experienced similar traumas can offer insights and a sense of belonging.
- **Embrace Self-Compassion.** Treat yourself with kindness and understanding as you navigate the challenges of recovery.
- **Practice Mindfulness**. Mindfulness techniques can

help you stay present and grounded as you explore your feelings and thoughts.

- **Explore Your Values**. Reflect on your core values and how they align with your post-trauma narrative.
- **Set Goals**. Establish new goals that reflect your evolving sense of meaning and purpose.
- **Engage in Acts of Kindness.** Helping others can foster a sense of purpose and meaning in your life.
- **Reflect on Your Resilience.** Acknowledge the strengths and resilience you've developed in response to your trauma.

The journey to finding meaning and purpose after trauma is a testament to the human spirit's resilience and capacity for growth. By engaging in the process of meaning-making, you can discover new depths of strength, purpose, and resilience. Through the active exploration of their values, relationships, and self-identity, survivors can emerge from the shadows of trauma into a brighter, more meaningful future.

Seeking Support

One of the most profound realizations when healing from trauma is that we don't heal in isolation but in community. The process of recovery is not just a solitary endeavor, but it's a collective journey that can be nurtured through seeking help, support, and guidance from others. The importance of reaching out to others in times of emotional distress cannot be overstated. As S. Kelly Harrel wisely stated, "Healing is not a path walked alone but one forged with the support of others" (Harrel, n.d.).

Trauma can leave you feeling isolated, overwhelmed, and unable to navigate your emotional terrain. Seeking help is the key to unlocking the healing potential that resides within each person. Here, we explore the importance of having a support system, discuss the various types of support available for trauma recovery, and provide guidance on how to build your own support network.

THE IMPORTANCE OF HAVING SUPPORT

The journey of healing from trauma often begins with the realization that the burden is too heavy to bear alone. Acknowledging that we need help and support is not a sign of weakness but a display of immense strength and courage. Here's why having a support system is of paramount importance:

- **Validation and Understanding:** Trauma can make individuals feel as if they're the only ones in the world experiencing such distressing emotions. Connecting with others who have faced similar challenges can provide validation and a profound sense of understanding.
- **Emotional Relief:** Sharing one's experiences, thoughts, and feelings with a trusted individual can offer emotional relief and alleviate the

overwhelming weight of trauma. It can be an essential part of the healing process.

- **Providing Perspective:** Friends, family members, mentors, or professionals can help you see your experiences from different angles, offering new perspectives and strategies for coping.

- **Guidance and Expertise:** Professionals have the training and knowledge to guide you through the complexities of trauma recovery. They can provide evidence-based techniques and therapies tailored to your unique needs.

- **Building Resilience:** Interacting with a support system can empower you to develop resilience and grit, enabling you to face your trauma with courage and determination.

- **Promoting Self-Care:** A support system often plays a crucial role in encouraging self-care. Loved ones, mentors, and professionals can guide you toward self-compassion and self-nurturing practices.

- **Preventing Isolation:** Isolation can exacerbate the negative effects of trauma. A strong support network can act as a buffer against isolation and offer a sense of belonging.

- **Empowering Decision-Making:** Support from others can help you make informed decisions about your recovery path. It provides a wealth of knowledge and expertise to draw upon.

TYPES OF SUPPORT FOR TRAUMA RECOVERY

Support for trauma recovery comes in various forms, and having a diverse support system can be incredibly beneficial.

- Family members and friends are often the first line of support. Their love, empathy, and understanding can be invaluable in providing emotional relief.
- Mentors are individuals who have navigated similar challenges and can offer guidance based on their experiences. They provide valuable insights and mentorship in your healing process.
- Spiritual leaders can also be a valuable support for those with a spiritual or religious background. These spiritual leaders can offer solace and support through faith-based guidance.
- Support groups bring together individuals who have faced similar traumatic experiences. These groups offer a space for sharing, understanding, and healing together.
- Helplines, such as suicide prevention hotlines, provide immediate assistance during critical moments of distress. These services offer a lifeline in times of crisis.

HOW TO BUILD YOUR SUPPORT SYSTEM

Building a support system is a dynamic process that can significantly contribute to your healing journey. Here are steps to consider when constructing your support network:

- **Identify Your Needs**. Reflect on your needs and preferences for support. Determine whether you require professional assistance, peer support, or the understanding of loved ones.
- **Engage with Mental Health Professionals**. If your trauma is deeply affecting your daily life, consider seeking help from mental health professionals such as therapists, counselors, or psychiatrists.
- **Reach Out to Loved Ones.** Share your experiences with your family and friends. Discuss your emotional struggles and tell them how they can support you effectively.
- **Join Support Groups.** Explore local or online support groups that cater to your specific types of trauma or emotional challenges. Connecting with individuals who share your experiences can be incredibly healing.
- **Seek Guidance from Mentors.** Identify individuals who have walked a similar path of recovery. Their guidance and mentorship can provide a sense of direction.

- **Utilize Crisis Helplines**: Keep contact information for crisis hotlines in case you ever need immediate assistance during moments of severe distress.
- **Practice Active Self-Care.** Engage in self-care practices that promote your well-being. Prioritize activities that reduce stress and contribute to your emotional stability.
- **Communicate Openly**. Maintain open and honest communication with your support network. Share your progress, setbacks, and any evolving needs.
- **Consider Professional Help**. If your trauma is deeply entrenched and affecting your daily life, it may be crucial to seek assistance from mental health professionals. Their expertise can prove targeted therapeutic interventions.
- **Patience and Persistence.** Building a support system takes time. Be patient and persistent in your efforts to connect with the right individuals who can support your healing journey effectively.

Recognize Your Strengths

The path to healing and personal growth is often laden with challenges. Amid trauma and its aftermath, you may feel overwhelmed, powerless, and even question your self-worth. However, it is crucial to recognize that every person possesses unique strengths and capabilities that can serve as a powerful foundation for recovery and transformation.

The recognition of your strengths is an integral part of your journey toward healing and growth. While the process may seem challenging, there are various ways to identify and harness your strengths effectively. The first step in recognizing your strengths is self-reflection. Take time to contemplate your experiences, accomplishments, and personal attributes. Consider the following questions:

- What have been some of my significant life achievements?
- When have I felt the most confident and capable?
- What personal qualities do I admire in myself?
- How have I coped with challenging situations in the past?

Self-reflection allows you to gain insights into your unique attributes and past successes, laying the foundation for recognizing your strengths. Several assessment tools are available to help you identify your strengths. The High5 Test, for example, is designed to pinpoint your top strengths (High-5Test, 2016). Such tools can provide you with a structured assessment, highlighting your unique abilities and attributes.

Often, those around us can offer valuable insights into our strengths. Seek feedback from friends, family, or mentors. Their perspectives can give you a broader view of your strengths and how you've positively impacted others. Recollect moments when you felt empowered, confident, and capable. Consider the circumstances, your actions, and the qualities you displayed during these high points. These experiences can offer valuable clues about our inherent strengths.

Recognize your values and passions. What are the causes, activities, or principles that you deeply care about? These reflect your inner strengths and the areas in which you naturally excel. Evaluate how you've coped with adversity; your ability to bounce back from difficult situations showcases your resilience, a powerful strength contributing to personal growth.

Reframing Your Narrative

Once you've identified your strengths, it's time to examine your trauma narrative and consider the importance of reframing it. A trauma narrative is the story you tell yourself about your traumatic experiences. It can be filled with pain, suffering, and victimhood. Reframing your narrative is about empowering yourself to view your experiences from a more constructive and growth-oriented perspective.

- **Acknowledge Your Growth**: Start by acknowledging the growth and resilience you've demonstrated in your journey. Recognize the strengths you've used to overcome challenges and how you've developed as a result of your experiences.
- **Focus on Post-Traumatic Growth**: Consider the concept of post-traumatic growth. This framework

emphasizes the potential for positive changes after trauma. Reframe your narrative to include the notion that your traumatic experiences have equipped you with unique strengths that you can leverage for personal development.

- **Challenge Negative Beliefs:** Identify and challenge any negative beliefs or self-perceptions that have arisen from your trauma narrative. Replace these with positive affirmations that highlight your strengths and potential.

- **Share Your Narrative:** Sharing your reframed narrative with a trusted friend, family member, or therapist can provide validation and support. They can help you identify strengths you may have overlooked.

- **Seek Professional Guidance:** As mentioned before, seeking assistance from a mental health professional to guide you through the process of reframing your narrative is of great importance. Therapy sessions are designed to help individuals restructure their narratives in a manner that fosters healing and growth.

By reframing your trauma narrative, you empower yourself to view experiences through a lens of strength, resilience, and potential. This transformation is a pivotal step in your journey toward recovery and growth.

Sustaining Long-Term Growth

Recognizing your strengths and reframing your narrative are essential components of your healing journey, but the path to sustained growth can be challenging. How do you stay motivated and committed to self-improvement over the long term? This section explores the ways you can maintain motivation, even when faced with setbacks.

Begin your journey of personal growth by setting realistic and achievable goals. Having clear objectives can provide direction and motivation. Acknowledge and celebrate the small victories along the way. Each achievement, no matter how minor, is a step closer to our larger goals. When you embrace a growth mindset, recognize that learning and growth are ongoing processes. Seek opportunities for continuous self-improvement.

Share your goals and progress with a trusted friend or mentor. Being accountable to someone else can boost motivation and commitment. Be kind and compassionate with yourself. Understand that setbacks are a natural part of growth. Self-compassion can help you recover from setbacks with resilience. Create a mental image of your future self. Visualizing the person you want to become can serve as a powerful motivator. Surround yourself with inspiration. Read books, listen to podcasts, or engage with individuals who motivate you to continue on your journey.

Furthermore, understand that setbacks are a part of any personal growth journey. Rather than seeing them as failures, view them as opportunities to learn and grow. Consider working with a therapist or counselor who specializes in trauma and personal growth. Professional guidance can provide valuable insights and strategies to sustain long-term growth. Recognizing your strengths, reframing your narrative, and sustaining long-term growth are pivotal in your journey toward healing and personal transformation.

Celebrate You

On the winding road of personal development and growth, celebrating your achievements and progress is not merely a frivolous act of self-indulgence; it is a crucial and transformative element worthy of exploration. Here are the reasons why celebrating your growth matters:

- **Boosting Motivation and Confidence:** Celebrating your achievements serves as a powerful motivator. It reinforces your self-belief and confidence, providing the impetus to continue working towards your goals. When you acknowledge your progress, no matter how small, you're more likely to stay committed to your journey or self-development.
- **Fostering Positivity:** Celebrating your growth brings positivity into your life. It shifts your focus from what you lack or haven't achieved to what you

have accomplished. Positivity acts as a catalyst for personal development, enhancing your emotional well-being and resilience.

- **Recognizing Self-Worth:** When you celebrate your achievements, you are essentially recognizing your self-worth. It affirms that you are deserving of acknowledgment and that your efforts are valuable. This sense of self-worth is foundational for long-term self-development.

- **Providing Milestones:** Celebrating your growth establishes meaningful milestones in your journey. These milestones allow you to track your progress and set new goals. They serve as markers, reminding you of how far you've come and where you intend to go.

- **Strengthening Resilience:** Acknowledging and celebrating your growth equips you with greater resilience. It helps you bounce back from setbacks, as you can reflect on your past achievements and draw strength from them. Resilience is a key asset for navigating the challenges that often accompany self-development.

WAYS TO CELEBRATE YOUR GROWTH

- **Reflection**: Take time to reflect on your journey and acknowledge your achievements. Consider keeping a journal where you write down your accomplishments, big or small. This practice allows you to see the progress you've made.
- **Small Wins:** Celebrate small wins as well as major milestones. Small victories are significant steps toward your long-term goals. Treat yourself when you accomplish them, whether with a small treat, a walk in the park, or some well-deserved relaxation.
- **Gratitude Practice:** Incorporate gratitude into your daily life. Express gratitude for your achievements and the progress you've made. Gratitude reinforces the positivity associated with celebrating your growth.
- **Share Your Success:** Don't hesitate to share yours with loved ones or close friends. Sharing your success not only provides a sense of pride but also fosters a supportive network that can cheer you on.
- **Reward Yourself:** Treat yourself to rewards when you reach certain milestones. These rewards can serve as incentives and reminders of the importance of celebrating your achievements.
- **Create a Vision Board:** Construct a vision board that represents your goals and aspirations. When you

achieve a goal, add a symbol or note to our board to mark your success.

- **Self-Affirmations:** Use positive affirmations to reinforce your sense of accomplishment. Affirmation can help you maintain a positive mindset and focus on your progress.
- **Capture the Moment:** Take photographs or create mementos that represent our growth and achievements. When you look back at these memories, you'll be reminded of our successes.
- **Set Future Goals:** Celebrating your growth is not just about looking back; it's also about looking forward. Use the motivation from your achievements to set new, challenging goals for your self-development journey.
- **Practice Self-Compassion:** Embrace self-compassion. Understand that growth is a process, and setbacks are natural. Treat yourself with kindness and forgiveness when you encounter challenges.

JOURNAL PROMPTS TO KEEP YOU ON AN UPWARD TRACK

Journaling can be a powerful tool to enhance your self-development journey. It allows you to delve deeper into your thoughts and experiences, fostering self-awareness and personal growth. Here are ten motivational journal prompts to inspire you:

- What are three accomplishments I'm proud of so far in my self-development journey?
- How do I feel when I celebrate my growth and achievements?
- What small win can I celebrate today to boost my motivation?
- Describe a moment in my life when I demonstrated resilience. How can I celebrate that?
- What is the self-affirmation I use to acknowledge my progress and capabilities.?
- How has gratitude positively impacted my self-development?
- What is my go-to method for self-compassion when I encounter setbacks?
- What goals have I set for my future self-development, and how do I plan to celebrate reaching them?
- How do I share my success with my support network? Why is it essential to me?
- What mementos or symbols represent my growth and achievements that I can incorporate into my vision board or life?

Celebrating your growth is an integral part of self-development, and these journal prompts can guide you in the process, helping you explore your achievements and goals. Celebrating your growth is not merely a joyful act of recognizing your achievement but an essential practice for long-term self-development. By taking the time to appreciate your progress, you reinforce your motivation, bolster your self-esteem, and cultivate a deep sense of purpose. It's through this self-affirmation that you build resilience and stay committed to the transformative journey of personal growth.

KEEPING THE GAME ALIVE

Now you have everything you need to heal from trauma, it's time to pass on your newfound knowledge and show other readers where they can find the same help.

Simply by leaving your honest opinion of this book on Amazon, you'll show other people recovering from trauma where they can find the information they need, and pass the passion for healing forward.

Thank you for your help. Trauma recovery is kept alive when we pass on our knowledge – and you're helping me do just that.

Scan the QR code below to leave your review:

CONCLUSION

We don't heal in isolation but in community.

— S. KELLEY HARREL

As we reach the culmination of this journey through trauma
and healing, it's essential to pause and reflect on the
profound insights and transformative knowledge you've
gained. In this concluding chapter, we'll sum up the core
messages of our exploration, emphasizing the key takeaways
that form the heart of our path to healing. We'll also share an
inspiring success story, reinforcing that recovery from
trauma is possible. Finally, we'll conclude with a powerful

call to action, urging you to embrace your growth, strength, and well-being potential.

UNVEILING THE CORE MESSAGE

Throughout this book, we've delved deep into the intricate landscape of trauma and its many facets. The core message that resounds in every chapter is a simple yet profound one: healing is not only possible but an innate human capacity. Regardless of the form trauma takes, regardless of the depths of your suffering, there is always hope. You can emerge from the shadows of trauma and rediscover the light within you.

Acknowledging your experiences is the first crucial step. By opening your heart and mind to the reality of your pain and struggles, you pave the way for recovery. At the same time, it may seem like an insurmountable mountain to climb, but remember that even partial recovery is a significant achievement. It's the initial spark of your resilience, and it matters immensely.

Celebrating Resilience: A Success Story

To illustrate the power of resilience and post-traumatic growth, let's turn to a remarkable success story. We often hear that trauma changes people, and it certainly does. Yet, it's the choices we make in the face of adversity that can define our future.

Meet Sarah. She experienced a traumatic childhood filled with adversity, abuse, and neglect. For years, she lived with the deep emotional scars of her past, believing that her trauma defined her identity. But Sarah decided that she would not be a prisoner of her past any longer.

She embarked on her healing journey, guided by therapy, support from loved ones, and a commitment to learning about herself. As she grappled with the darkness of her past, she discovered a remarkable strength within her. She acknowledged her suffering, sought help, and diligently engaged in therapeutic techniques like narrative exposure therapy. Through this transformative process, she began to rewrite her narrative.

Sarah found solace in the support of others, both from her family and her friends, as well as a peer support group. It was within these connections that she realized:

Sarah's resilience was a testament to the power of human connection. Her journey was not without its challenges. There were days when her past seemed unbearable, when her motivation waned, and when she questioned her path. But she persevered, tapping into her newfound resilience and a growth mindset that fueled her progress.

One day, while reflecting on her journey, Sarah realized that her trauma had not solely left her with scars. It had given her strengths too. Through therapy and self-reflection, she identified her innate qualities, such as empathy, perseverance, and courage. These strengths guided her toward post-traumatic growth.

Sarah's story exemplifies the central message of this book-healing is possible, and post-traumatic growth is achievable. She overcame the chains of her past and emerged stronger, more resilient, and with a deeper understanding of herself.

A CALL TO ACTION

As you reach the end of this book, our mission is not just to provide you with knowledge but to empower you to take action. The road to post-traumatic growth and personal renewal awaits you, and it's a journey worth embarking upon. A life filled with growth, strength, and well-being is within your reach.

Your journey to healing and post-traumatic growth is a powerful narrative of self-discovery and transformation. As you stand at the intersection of your past and the boundless potential of your future, you hold the key to your healing. Here are the vital actions you can take to move forward on your path to recovery and growth.

- **Acknowledge Your Trauma:** If you haven't already, begin your journey by acknowledging the significance of your experiences and the profound impact they've had on your life. Understand that it's more than acceptable to seek help and support.

- **Seek Help:** Always remember you don't have to traverse the winding road to healing in solitude. Reach out for assistance from professionals, support groups, trusted friends, or your family. Recognize the immense strength found in the power of community on your journey.

- **Reflect on Your Belief:** Cultivate a growth mindset by engaging in self-reflection. Dive into the depths of your beliefs and attitudes. Understand that personal development is an ongoing voyage, and within you lies the capacity to adapt and grow.

- **Find Meaning and Purpose:** Uncover the beauty of the meaning-making model to discover purpose within your journey. Explore the potential for transformation that adversity and suffering hold. Reflect on how these experiences can shape your path.

- **Celebrate Your Growth:** Remember, no matter how seemingly small, every step you take toward healing is a notable achievement. Celebrate your accomplishments with pride. These milestones collectively signify your journey of strength and resilience.

- **Stay Motivated:** Maintaining long-term growth involves nurturing the motivation to persist on your path of self-improvement. Embrace life's challenges as opportunities for your growth and renewal.

- **Recognize Your Strengths:** Delve deep into the realms of self-exploration to uncover your unique personal qualities and attributes. Identify your strengths as the invaluable tools that will enable you to overcome adversity.

- **Reframe Your Narrative:** Practice the art of narrative reframing. Transform the way you receive your trauma and personal story. Reconstruct your narrative with resilience, strength, and growth potential.

- **Journal Your Journey:** Harness the profound potential of journal prompts to inspire self-reflection and ignite personal growth. Your journal can serve as a canvas for your journey and a testament to your resilience.

- **Seek the Support of Others:** Construct a robust support system, one that may include your loved ones, mentors, peer support groups, and crisis hotlines. These connections can be invaluable guides on your path to recovery.

- **Continue Learning:** Understand that education and self-improvement are perpetual processes. Maintain your commitment to personal growth, resilience, and overall well-being. Approach each day as an opportunity to learn, evolve, and thrive.

- **Celebrate You:** Embrace the practices of celebrating your personal growth and accomplishments. Even the smallest steps forward are worth acknowledging. This celebration can be the fuel that drives your motivation and reinforces your journey of healing and post-traumatic growth.

Incorporate these actions into your healing process as you move forward with newfound purpose and resilience. Your journey is a testament to your strength and your capacity for growth.

A life filled with growth, strength, and well-being is waiting for you. Break free from trauma and start your journey to healing today. Remember that your story, like Sarah's and so many others, is one of resilience and transformation waiting to be written.

If this book has helped you gain a deeper insight into your experiences of trauma and how you can begin healing, we kindly request that you share your thoughts in a review. Your review can guide and support others seeking to triumph over trauma. We are grateful for your contribution and look forward to hearing your story of growth and renewal.

As you move forward on your path to healing and self-discovery, know that you are not alone. The journey may be challenging, but with determination, resilience, and the support of others, you have the power to heal and emerge from your experiences of trauma as a stronger and more resilient version of yourself. The seeds of post-traumatic growth are within you, waiting to flourish. Embrace the possibilities, cherish the lessons, and continue your remarkable journey toward a brighter, healthier future!

GLOSSARY

Journal Prompts: Journal prompts are questions or statements designed to stimulate self-reflection and encourage personal growth when used as writing prompts in a journal.

Celebration of Growth: Celebration of growth is recognizing and acknowledging one's accomplishments and progress along the journey of trauma recovery.

Cognitive Behavioral Therapy (CBT): CBT is a therapeutic approach aimed at changing negative thought patterns and behaviors. It's effective in treating PTSD and other trauma-related disorders.

Exposure Therapies: Exposure therapies involve confronting distressing thoughts, memories, or situations related to trauma as a means of reducing their emotional impact.

Imaginal Exposure: Imaginal exposure is a technique in which individuals mentally revisit their traumatic experiences by creating a detailed narrative of the events.

Interoceptive Exposure: Interoceptive exposure is used in treating anxiety disorders, including PTSD. It involves inducing and tolerating the physical sensations associated with anxiety triggers.

In-Vivo Exposure: In-vivo exposure involves facing real-life situations or triggers related to trauma, gradually reducing the emotional distress associated with them.

Meaning-Making Model: The meaning-making model is a framework for finding purpose and understanding in the aftermath of trauma.

Mindset: Mindset is one's fundamental beliefs and attitudes that shape how they perceive and respond to challenges, including growth mindset and fixed mindset.

Motivation: Motivation is the driving force that compels individuals to pursue self-improvement and personal development.

Narrative Exposure Therapy: Narrative exposure therapy is a method used to help individuals process traumatic memories by verbally recounting their traumatic experiences.

Narrative Reframing: Narrative reframing involves reevaluating and altering how individuals perceive and tell their trauma stories to promote healing and growth.

Post-Traumatic Growth: Post-traumatic growth refers to the positive psychological changes that can result from experiencing trauma, such as increased resilience, personal development, and a deeper appreciation of life.

Post-Traumatic Stress Disorder (PTSD): PTSD is a mental health condition that can develop after a person experiences a traumatic event. Symptoms include flashbacks, nightmares, and severe anxiety.

Prolonged Exposure: Prolonged exposure is a therapeutic technique for treating PTSD, where individuals systematically confront their trauma-related memories, triggers, and thoughts.

Resilience: Resilience is the ability to bounce back from adversity, trauma, or stress, demonstrating the capacity to adapt and recover effectively.

Review: A review is a thoughtful assessment or evaluation of the book, which can help others seek insights into trauma and healing.

Self-Reflection: Self-reflection is examining one's thoughts, emotions, and experiences to gain insight and understanding.

Strengths: Strengths are personal qualities, skills, and attributes that can be harnessed to overcome adversity and achieve personal growth.

Support System: A support system comprises loved ones, friends, mentors, or professionals who provide emotional, psychological, and practical assistance during trauma recovery.

Trauma: Trauma refers to the psychological and emotional response to a distressing event or series of events, which may have long-lasting effects on a person's mental well-being.

Therapeutic Techniques: These are various approaches and methods used in therapy to help individuals cope with and heal from trauma.

REFERENCES

A self-care plan for survivors. (2021, April 23). Life Insight Therapy Collective. https://life-insight.com/a-self-care-plan-for-survivors/

ABC News. (2011, November 30). *The stuff of dreams: How sleep eases emotional trauma.* ABC News. https://abcnews.go.com/Technology/dreams-ease-effects-trauma-post-traumatic-stress-disorder/story?id=15052034

About NST. (2023, April 10). https://cns.edu/about-nst/

ajt2018. (2020, June 9). *5 reasons it's imperative to attend follow-up medical and mental health appointments after an accident.* AJ Therapy Center. https://ajtherapycenter.com/5-reasons-its-imperative-to-attend-follow-up-medical-and-mental-health-appointments-after-an-accident/

Allardice, L. (2021, March 27). Maggie O'Farrell: *'Severe illness refigures you – it's like passing through a fire.'* The Guardian. https://www.theguardian.com/books/2021/mar/27/maggie-ofarrell-severe-illness-refigures-you-its-like-passing-through-a-fire

Andrea. (2023, June 24). *5 ways to identify your strengths and what you're good at!* Tracking Happiness. https://www.trackinghappiness.com/how-to-identify-your-strengths/

Applebury, G. (2021, January 8). *The dual process model of grief in simple terms.* LoveToKnow. https://www.lovetoknow.com/life/grief-loss/dual-process-model-grief-simple-terms#:~:text=The%20dual%20process%20model%20of%20grief%20is%20a

Araminta. (2022, April 8). *Shame and trauma.* Khiron Clinics. https://khironclinics.com/blog/shame-and-trauma/

Araminta. (2023, March 17). *Improving emotional regulation: tips and techniques.* Khiron Clinics. https://khironclinics.com/blog/improving-emotional-regulation/

Articles - Brilliantio. (n.d.). B. https://brilliantio.com/articles/

Assault survivors advocacy program. (n.d.). University of Northern Colorado. https://www.unco.edu/assault-survivors-advocacy-program/

Audrey's Blog - Audrey Jolly Therapy Registered Psychotherapist, Integral healing,. (n.d.). https://www.audreyjollytherapy.com/site/blog/

Bailey, J. R., & Rehman, S. (2022, March 4). *Don't underestimate the power of self-reflection.* Harvard Business Review. https://hbr.org/2022/03/dont-underestimate-the-power-of-self-reflection

Barriers to physical activity. (n.d.). Physiopedia. https://www.physio-pedia.com/Barriers_to_Physical_Activity

Bastos, F. (2023, January 25). *4 reasons you should practice mindfulness for your PTSD.* MindOwl. https://mindowl.org/mindfulness-ptsd/?expand_article=1

Baum, E. (2022, December 16). *How alcohol affects mental health.* 7 Summit Pathways. https://7summitpathways.com/blog/how-alcohol-affects-mental-health/

Bhati, K. (2022, April 23). *What are the 5 stages of post traumatic growth? How to get started?* Calm Sage. https://www.calmsage.com/post-traumatic-growth/

Body awareness in survivors of trauma. (n.d.). Physiopedia. https://www.physio-pedia.com/Body_Awareness_in_Survivors_of_Trauma?utm_source=physiopedia&utm_medium=search&utm_campaign=ongoing_internal

Bonura, D. (n.d.). *Spirituality and trauma.* The Warrior's Journey. https://thewarriorsjourney.org/challenges/spirituality-trauma/

Boyd, J. E., Lanius, R. A., & McKinnon, M. C. (2018). Mindfulness-based treatments for posttraumatic stress disorder: a review of the treatment literature and neurobiological evidence. *Journal of Psychiatry & Neuroscience, 43(1),* 7–25. https://doi.org/10.1503/jpn.170021

Brickel, R. E. (2019, April 24). *9 signs you need better self-care and may be a trauma survivor.* PsychAlive. https://www.psychalive.org/9-signs-you-need-better-self-care-and-may-be-a-trauma-survivor/

Brodsky, S. (2022, September 16). *25 journal prompts to help you get unstuck.* Wondermind. https://www.wondermind.com/article/motivational-journal-prompts/

Bullock, B. G. (2019, July 11). *The science of how mindfulness relieves post traumatic stress.* Mindful. https://www.mindful.org/the-science-of-how-mindfulness-relieves-post-traumatic-stress/

Butler, L. (2019, October 28). *Developing your self-care plan*. University at Buffalo. https://socialwork.buffalo.edu/resources/self-care-starter-kit/developing-your-self-care-plan.html

CBT worksheets, handouts, and skills-development audio: Therapy resources for mental health professionals. (2023, September 12). Psychology Tools. https://www.psychologytools.com/downloads/cbt-worksheets-and-therapy-resources/

Center for healing shame. (n.d.). Center for Healing Shame. https://healing shame.com/

Center, K. (2018, October 22). *How do I start a relationship with a higher power?* The Kimberly Center. https://kimberlycenter.com/addiction/start-rela tionship-higher-power/

Clinical practice guideline for the treatment of posttraumatic stress disorder (PTSD) in adults. (2023, March). Clinical Practice Guideline for the Treatment of Postraumatic Stress Disorder. https://www.apa.org/ptsd-guideline/

Cognitive behavioral therapy (CBT). (2018, June 5). GoodTherapy https://www.goodtherapy.org/learn-about-therapy/types/cognitive-behavioral-therapy

Conlon, K. (2021, March 25). *5 trauma release exercises you can try at home!* Cohesive Therapy NYC. https://cohesivetherapynyc.com/blog/5-trauma-release-exercises-you-can-try-at-home/

Cooks-Campbell, A. (2022, July 15). Triggers: learn to recognize and deal with them. *BetterUp*. https://www.betterup.com/blog/triggers

Cooper, B. (2016, September 1). *3 science-backed ways to boost your motivation (even when you don't feel like working)*. Zapier. https://zapier.com/blog/stay-motivated-at-work/

Cuccurullo, L., & Joyce, J. (n.d.). *In vivo exposures for prolonged exposure therapy during a pandemic*. U.S. Department of Veterans Affairs. https://www.ptsd.va.gov/covid/covid_pe_invivo.asp#:~:text=During%20in%20-vivo%20exposure%2C%20patients

Cuncic, A. (2023, May 5). *How to develop and use self-regulation in your life*. Verywell Mind. https://www.verywellmind.com/how-you-can-practice-self-regulation-4163536

Danylchuk, L. (2015, June 11). These 5 domains of posttraumatic growth can help you thrive. Good *Therapy Blog*. https://www.goodtherapy.org/

blog/these-5-domains-of-posttraumatic-growth-can-help-you-thrive-0611155

Davis, A. (2023a, March 11). *72 trauma affirmations to support your healing journey.* Ambitiously Alexa. https://ambitiouslyalexa.com/trauma-affirmations/

Davis, A. (2023b, August 3). *80 motivating self improvement journal prompts.* Ambitiously Alexa. https://ambitiouslyalexa.com/self-improvement-journal-prompts/

Davis, S. (2020, January 20). *The mental health benefits of prayer.* CPTSDFoundation.org. https://cptsdfoundation.org/2020/01/20/the-mental-health-benefits-of-prayer/

Doll, K. (2019, March 23). *23 resilience building activities & exercises for adults.* PositivePsychology.com. https://positivepsychology.com/resilience-activities-exercises/

Duong, M. (2021, January 11). *How to make meaning after traumatic events.* Committee for Children. https://www.cfchildren.org/blog/2021/01/meaning-making-after-trauma-winter-well-being/

Dweck, C. (2015a, March 2). Carol Dweck: A summary of the two mindsets. *Farnam Street.* https://fs.blog/carol-dweck-mindset/#:~:text=In%20this%20mindset%2C%20the%20hand

Eatough, E. (2021, August 23). Seeking help for your mental health is brave. And beneficial. *BetterUp.* https://www.betterup.com/blog/seeking-help

Eatough, E. (2023, September 23). 41 motivation tips to keep you moving forward. *BetterUp.* https://www.betterup.com/blog/how-to-stay-motivated

EMDR, somatic experiencing, brainspotting. (n.d.). Mckinney Counseling & Recovery. https://intensivehope.com/emdr-somatic-experiencing/

Emotional dysregulation: How to feel about managing feelings. (n.d.). Cleveland Clinic. https://my.clevelandclinic.org/health/symptoms/25065-emotional-dysregulation

Emotional intelligence: Definition and 5 ways you can improve yours! (2022, February 14). Professional Leadership Institute. https://professionalleadershipinstitute.com/resources/emotional-intelligence-definition-and-5-ways-you-can-improve-yours/

Ertel, A. (2023, February 2). *The different types of trauma explained.* Talkspace. https://www.talkspace.com/blog/types-of-trauma/

Eshkevari, L., Permaul, E., & Mulroney, S. E. (2013). Acupuncture blocks cold stress-induced increases in the hypothalamus–pituitary–adrenal axis in the rat. *Journal of Endocrinology, 217(1)*, 95–104. https://doi.org/10.1530/joe-12-0404

ESV Bible. (2001). ESV Bible online. https://www.esv.org/verses/PSALM%2034%3A18/

Explore LinkedIn. (n.d.). www.linkedin.com. https://www.linkedin.com/pulse/topics/home/

Explore therapy. (n.d.). GoodTherapy. https://www.goodtherapy.org/explore-therapy.html

Expressive trauma integration | Psychology Today. (n.d.). www.psychologytoday.com. https://www.psychologytoday.com/us/blog/expressive-trauma-integration

Fazeli Fard, M. (2019, August 29). *How movement therapy can heal traumatic stress.* Experience Life. https://experiencelife.lifetime.life/article/how-movement-therapy-can-heal-traumatic-stress/

Ferrara, D . (2023, March 20). Trauma denial: What it is and when it's time to address it. *Calmerry Blog.* https://calmerry.com/blog/grief-and-loss/trauma-denial-why-it-can-help-and-hurt-your-healing/

Fielding, S. (2023, July 24). *What are trauma release exercises & do they work?* Charlie Health. https://www.charliehealth.com/post/trauma-release-exercises

Fort Behavioral Health. (2023, February 20). *How trauma can impact your mental health.* Fort Behavioral Health. https://www.fortbehavioral.com/addiction-recovery-blog/how-trauma-can-impact-your-mental-health/

The #4mind4body challenge. (n.d.). Mental Health America. https://www.mhanational.org/4mind4body-challenge

Four misconceptions about trauma. (n.d.). Akua Mind & Body. https://akuamindbody.com/four-misconceptions-about-trauma/

Friedman, D. (2022, July 7). *The healing power of strength training.* The New York Times. https://www.nytimes.com/2022/07/07/well/move/weight-lifting-ptsd-trauma.html?searchResultPosition=3

Gilbert, A. (2022, October 19). *The top 5 most effective trauma processing techniques.* Soberish. https://www.soberish.co/trauma-processing-techniques/

Gilbert, A. (2023, July 15). *12 signs of repressed childhood trauma in adults*. Soberish. https://www.soberish.co/signs-of-repressed-childhood-trauma-in-adults/

Glauser, E. (2012, November 27). *Trauma, stress, and restorative sleep*. Psychology Today. https://www.psychologytoday.com/intl/blog/golden-slumbers/201211/trauma-stress-and-restorative-sleep

Goldsteien, S. (2023, September 26). *Trauma 2020: Where we wear it and how we treat it*. Pacific College. https://www.pacificcollege.edu/news/blog/2021/03/04/trauma-2020-where-we-wear-it-and-how-we-treat-it

Gordon, J. (2020, January 1). *The trauma-healing*. TAPS. https://www.taps.org/articles/25-4/trauma-healing-diet

Greenwald, R. (2021, November 3). *Exercise to support trauma healing*. Trauma Institute & Child Trauma Institute. https://www.ticti.org/exercise/

GregW. (2020, August 4). *Shame: why does it come from trauma?* Quest Psychology Services. https://questpsychologyservices.co.uk/shame-why-does-it-come-from-trauma/

The Guest House. (2018, July 9). *The role of a higher power in trauma recovery*. The Guest House. https://www.theguesthouseocala.com/the-role-of-a-higher-power-in-trauma-recovery/

The Guest House. (2020a, November 22). *Creating a healthy mindset in recovery | The Guest House*. The Guest House. https://www.theguesthouseocala.com/the-impact-of-a-healthy-mindset-in-recovery/

The Guest House. (2020b, November 22) *The impact of a healthy mindset in recovery*. The Guest House. https://www.theguesthouseocala.com/the-impact-of-a-healthy-mindset-in-recovery/

Guy Evans, O. (2023, November 9). *Exposure therapy: definition, techniques, interventions*. Simply Psychology. https://www.simplypsychology.org/exposure-therapy.html

Harrel, S. K. (n.d.). *S. Kelley Harrel quotes*. Goodreads. https://www.goodreads.com/quotes/616038-we-don-t-heal-in-isolation-but-in-community

Harselle, S. (2022, April 25). *What is somatic trauma therapy?* Verywell Health. https://www.verywellhealth.com/somatic-trauma-therapy-5218970

Heal your trauma with nutritious foods. (2018, January 22). Anya Light. https://

anyalight.com/2018/01/22/heal-trauma-with-healing-foods/

HealthMatch Staff. (2022, September 1). *A guide to the different types of trauma.* HealthMatch. https://healthmatch.io/ptsd/different-types-of-trauma#overview

Herdocia-Oria, N. (2020, September 29). *10 practical ways to stay motivated on your self-improvement journey.* Coral Gables Counseling Center. https://www.coralgablescounseling.com/10-practical-ways-to-stay-motivated-on-your-self-improvement-journey/

High5Test. (2016). *Free strengths test | find your unique talents and character traits.* High 5 Test. https://high5test.com/

Hing, N. N. F., & Bhangu, A. (2021, July 30). *Physical activity and sleep may have synergistic effects on health.* 2 Minute Medicine. https://www.2minutemedicine.com/physical-activity-and-sleep-may-have-synergistic-effects-on-health/

Ho, L. (2023, February 3). *How to celebrate small wins to achieve big goals.* Lifehack. https://www.lifehack.org/396379/how-celebrate-small-wins-achieve-big-goals

Holcomb, B. (2020, January 29). *Foods for healing trauma through nutrition - BlackDoctor.org - Where Wellness & Culture Connect.* BlackDoctor.org. https://blackdoctor.org/foods-for-healing-trauma-through-nutrition/

Hood, J. (2018, December 20). *The importance of self-care after trauma.* Highland Springs. https://highlandspringsclinic.org/the-importance-of-self-care-after-trauma/

How acupuncture has helped some PTSD sufferers. (n.d.). Ptsd UK. https://www.ptsduk.org/acupuncture/

How celebrating your success helps in self-improvement? (n.d.). Happiom. https://www.happiom.com/celebrate-success/

How to be more you: reframing your story. (2022, April 8). Iris Higgins Hypnotherapy. https://irishiggins.com/how-to-be-more-you-reframing-your-story/

How to build well-being in the digital age. (2019). The Berkeley Well-Being Institute. https://www.berkeleywellbeing.com/

How to have compassion towards yourself and others. (n.d.). Navigating This Space. https://navigatingthisspace.com/how-to-have-compassion-self-compassion/

How trauma affects our daily lives. (2023, February 27). Pyramid Healthcare. https://www.pyramid-healthcare.com/the-different-ways-trauma-affects-our-lives/

How trauma changes the brain. (2022, December 7). Neuroscience News. https://www.neurosciencenews.com/salience-network-trauma-22026/

Howell, J. (2022, November 12). *Self-conscious emotions: the role of shame and guilt in trauma.* Luminous Counseling. https://www.luminouscounseling.org/blog/self-conscious-emotions-the-role-of-shame-and-guilt-in-trauma/

Howland, G. J. (n.d.). *Ways to conquer PTSD – why diet really matters!* Food & Mood centre. https://foodandmoodcentre.com.au/2018/09/ways-to-conquer-ptsd-why-diet-really-matters/

Innercamp. (2022, July 5). *Somatic psychotherapy tools: resourcing, titration and pendulation.* InnerCamp. https://innercamp.com/somatic-psychotherapy-tools-resourcing-titration-and-pendulation/

Janet. (2023, January 26). *Trauma sensitive meditation - the power of self-nurturing.* Tara Brach. https://www.tarabrach.com/trauma-sensitive-mindfulness/

Johansson, M. (2021, January 12). *What is emotional resilience and how to develop this important trait.* Maya Johansson, LMFT. https://wellsanfrancisco.com/what-is-emotional-resilience-and-how-to-develop-this-important-trait/

Jones, H. (n.d.). *Horacio Jones quotes.* Goodreads. https://www.goodreads.com/quotes/7569565-instead-of-saying-i-m-damaged-i-m-broken-i-have-trust

Jones, R. (2022, November 24). *75 childhood trauma quotes to get past your trauma.* Happier Human. https://www.happierhuman.com/childhood-trauma-quotes/

Kara. (2022, August 19). *Trauma denial: What is it and how can you work through it?* Kara Counseling. https://hartzellcounseling.com/trauma-denial-what-is-it-and-how-can-you-work-through-it/

Keller, C. (2022, April 28). Your 5-minute read on restorative sleep. Healthline. https://www.healthline.com/health/5-minute-read-on-restorative-sleep

King James Bible. (2017). King James Bible Online. https://www.kingjames

bibleonline.org/bible-verses-like_Psalms-34-18/ (Original work published 1769)

King James Bible. (2017). King James Bible Online. https://www.kingjames bibleonline.org/bible-verses-like_Psalms-34-18/ (Original work published 1769)

Klein, S. (2018, April 10). *How to sleep better: 37 hacks.* CNN Health. https:// edition.cnn.com/2015/05/14/health/sleep-hacks/index.html

Kress, H. (n.d.). *Home.* Dr. Anna Kress. https://drannakress.com/

Kristenson, S. (2022, August 25). *101 affirmations for people dealing with ptsd.* Happier Human. https://www.happierhuman.com/affirmations-ptsd/

Krouse, L. (2022, August 4). . *Here's what "processing" trauma really means—and how it helps you heal.* SELF. https://www.self.com/story/processing-trauma

Kulkarni, S. (2020, February 12). *7 Early signs that indicate you need to focus on self-care.* Editage Insights. https://www.editage.com/insights/7-early-signs-that-indicate-you-need-to-focus-on-self-care?refer=insights-search-posts

LaGuardia, G. (2023, May 29). *8 reasons why you should face your trauma.* Beachside Rehab. https://www.beachsiderehab.com/blog/8-reasons-why-you-should-face-your-trauma/

Laurence, E. (2020, June 25). *How nutrition can be used to support trauma recovery.* Well+Good. https://www.wellandgood.com/nutrition-trauma-recovery/

Lawrence, J. (2020, October 26). *Resilience and the adversities of life.* In Equilibrium. https://www.in-equilibrium.co.uk/resilience-and-the-adversities-of-life/

Lebow, H. I. (021, November 12). Trauma denial: How to recognize it and why it matters. Psych Central. https://psychcentral.com/blog/denial-of-trauma-signs#how-to-

Lebow, H. I. (2021, December 22). What is post-traumatic growth?. Psych Central. https://psychcentral.com/health/post-traumatic-growth

Levine, P. (n.d.). *Peter Levine quotes.* Truama 101. https://trauma101.com/what-is-trauma/#:

Loggins, B. (2022, April 26). *What is hakomi therapy?* Verywell Mind. https:// www.verywellmind.com/what-is-hakomi-therapy-5217674

Looney, S. (2022, September 23). *Big picture thinking and zooming out: Why we need it and how to develop it.* Sonya Looney. https://sonyalooney.com/ig-picture-thinking-why-we-need-it-and-how-to-develop-it/

Lovering, N. (2021, October 14). *Interoceptive exposure for anxiety: Does it work?* Psych Central. https://psychcentral.com/anxiety/interoceptive-exposure-for-treating-anxiety

Mairanz, A. (2019, November 14). *Growth mindset & four ways to celebrate growth | NYC Therapist.* Empower Your Mind Therapy. https://eymther apy.com/blog/celebrate-growth-mindset/

Making a trauma-informed self-care plan. (n.d.). http://www.pacwrc.pitt.edu/ Curriculum/313_MngngImpctTrmtcStrssChldWlfrPrfssnl/hndts/ HO06_MkngTrmInfrmdSlfCrPln.pdf

Marschall, A. (2023, May 20). *The role of the amygdala in human behavior and emotion.* Verywell Mind. https://www.verywellmind.com/the-role-of-the-amygdala-in-human-behavior-and-emotion-7499223

Martin, S. (2018, September 18). *How to stay motivated through the ups & downs of change.* Live Well with Sharon Martin. https://www.livewell withsharonmartin.com/how-to-stay-motivated-personal-growth/

Martinson, L. (2021, July 6). *My journey from trauma and abuse to healing.* KnoWEwell. https://www.knowewell.com/written-content/my-jour ney-trauma-and-abuse-healing

Meehan, J. (n.d.). *Identifying your strengths.* Restorative Counseling. https:// rcchicago.org/identifying-your-strengths/

Menakem, R. ((n.d.). *Resmaa Menakem quotes.* Inspiring Quotes. https://www. inspiringquotes.com/14-quotes-about-overcoming-trauma/Y0C44i6-xQAH_jL4

Merriam-Webster. (n.d.). Hypervigilance. In *Merriam-Webster dictionary.* Retrieved November 18, 2023. https://www.merriam-webster.com/ dictionary/hypervigilance

Molyneux, S. (n.d.). *Stefan Molyneux quotes.* Goodreads. https://www. goodreads.com/quotes/1307479-there-s-no-weakness-as-great-as-false-strength

Miezio, A. (2023, March 6). *Know the 7 types of trauma like a psychotherapist.* Psychedelic.support. https://psychedelic.support/resources/know-the-7-types-of-trauma-like-a-psychotherapist/

Morey-Nase, C. (2021, March 23). Mindfulness, traumatic stress & best practice guidelines. Smiling Mind. https://blog.smilingmind.com.au/mindfulness-traumatic-stress-best-practice-guidelines

Muk, K. (2007, January 13). *How to stay motivated to work on self-improvement – Integrative Systemic Coaching*. https://iscmentoring.eu/km/personal-growth/how-to-stay-motivated-to-work-on-self-improvement/

Murphy, J. (2022, April 25). *How to use mindfulness to compassionately cope with trauma*. Healthline. https://www.healthline.com/health/how-trauma-informed-mindfulness-helps-me-heal-from-the-past-and-cope-with-the-present

Nash, J. (2022, January 21). *24 best self-soothing techniques and strategies for adults*. PositivePsychology.com. https://positivepsychology.com/self-soothing/

Nathanson, A. (n.d.). *Nine ways to navigate your trauma*. My Wellbeing https://mywellbeing.com/therapy-101/nine-ways-to-navigate-your-trauma

Neurobiology of trauma. (n.d.). Evergreen Psychotherapy Center. https://evergreenpsychotherapycenter.com/neurobiology-trauma/

Neurogenic yoga. (n.d.). Jo Hamilton Yoga. https://johamiltonyoga.co.uk/neurogenic-yoga/

NeURoscience. (n.d.). URMC Newsroom. https://www.urmc.rochester.edu/news/publications/neuroscience/

Nikravan Hayes, L. (2023, October 5). *Post-traumatic stress disorder (PTSD)*. Talkspace. https://www.talkspace.com/mental-health/conditions/post-traumatic-stress-disorder/

OAC Staff. (2023, May 1). *What is anxiety? The OCD & anxiety center*. https://theocdandanxietycenter.com/what-is-anxiety/

OCD Center Los Angeles. (2016, April 25). *Imaginal exposure for OCD and anxiety*. OCD Center of Los Angeles. https://ocdla.com/imaginal-exposure-ocd-anxiety-4847

Olanubi, D. (n.d.). *Dele Olanubi quotes*. Medium. https://medium.com/an-idea/dipping-back-in-healing-trauma-is-not-a-straight-line-4e370d22af4

Page, P. (n.d.). *Exercise and post-traumatic stress disorder*. NASM. https://blog.nasm.org/exercise-and-post-traumatic-stress-disorder

Palms, P. F. (2022, August 22). *5 self-soothing techniques for PTSD.* Promises Five Palms. https://www.my5palms.com/addiction-blog/5-self-soothing-techniques-for-ptsd/

Pedersen, T. (2021, August 18). All about somatic therapy. *Psych Central.* https://psychcentral.com/blog/how-somatic-therapy-can-help-patients-suffering-from-psychological-trauma

Perper, R. (2020, July 10). *How to be patient with yourself and others in a changing world.* Therapy Changes. https://therapychanges.com/blog/2020/07/how-to-be-patient-with-yourself-and-others-in-a-changing-world/

Peterson, T. J. (2023, August 25). *Sensorimotor psychotherapy: How it works, cost, & what to expect.* Choosing Therapy. https://www.choosingtherapy.com/sensorimotor-psychotherapy/

Phang, H. (2020, October 5). *How to do a squat: Ideal foot angle & width.* Propel Physiotherapy. https://propelphysiotherapy.com/exercise/how-to-do-a-squat-ideal-foot-angle-width/

Phillips, A. (2022, June 21). *Spiritual healing childhood trauma: 5 holistic exercises to overcome traumatic events.* TheMentalDesk.com https://www.thementaldesk.com/spiritual-healing-childhood-trauma/

Pillay, K., & Eagle, G. (2021). The case for mindfulness interventions for traumatic stress in high violence, low resource settings. *Current Psychology, 40(6),* 40(6). Research Gate. https://doi.org/10.1007/s12144-019-00177-1

Post-traumatic growth. (n.d.). Psychology Today. https://www.psychologytoday.com/us/basics/post-traumatic-growth#:~:text=Post-%20Traumatic%20Growth%20is%20the%20positive%20psychological%20change

PTSD: National center for PTSD. (n.d.). U.S. Department of Veterans Affairs. https://www.ptsd.va.gov/index.asp

Power of Positivity. (2023, May 21). *8 ways to beat ADHD (without medicine).* Power of Positivity. https://www.powerofpositivity.com/8-ways-to-beat-adhd-without-medicine/

The power of Reiki in healing trauma. (n.d.). Mutual Ground. https://mutualground.org/blog/the-power-of-reiki-in-healing-trauma

Prayers for healing emotional wounds. (n.d.). Knowing Jesus. https://prayer.knowing-jesus.com/prayer/prayers-for-healing-emotional-wounds-

1446

Problem vs. solution focused thinking. JZero Solutions. https://jzeroblog.com/2016/09/14/problem-vs-solution-oriented-thinking/

Psych Central Guest Author. (2014, September 18). New study examines the effects of prayer on mental health. *Psych Central.* https://psychcentral.com/blog/new-study-examines-the-effects-of-prayer-on-mental-health#1

Psychology India Magazine. (2023, January 11). *Nutrition for trauma recovery.* Psychology India Magazine. https://www.psychology.net.in/nutrition-for-trauma-recovery/

Psychology Today Staff. (n.d.). *Emotion Regulation | Psychology Today.* Psychology Today. https://www.psychologytoday.com/us/basics/emotion-regulation

Psychology Today Staff. (n.d.). *Prolonged exposure therapy.* Psychology Today. https://www.psychologytoday.com/za/therapy-types/prolonged-exposure-therapy

Psychology Today Staff. (n.d.). *Trauma.* Psychology Today. https://www.psychologytoday.com/us/basics/trauma

PTSD awareness day 2023. (2023). EML. https://www.eml.com.au/news-community/latest-news/ptsd-awareness-day-2023/

Quinn, D. (2022, December 23). *Exposure and response prevention: 5+ ERP techniques.* Sandstone Care. https://www.sandstonecare.com/blog/exposure-response-prevention-erp/

Quinn, D. (2023, August 3). *Types of trauma: The 7 most common types & their impacts.* Sandstone Care. https://www.sandstonecare.com/blog/types-of-trauma/

Quinn, D. (2023, May 25). *Somatic therapy: understanding the mind-body connection.* Sandstone Care. https://www.sandstonecare.com/blog/somatic-therapy/

Quirke, M. G. (2023, April 11). *How do you begin processing trauma?* Michael G. Quirke, MFT. https://michaelgquirke.com/how-do-you-begin-processing-trauma/

Ramirez-Duran, D. (2020, November 11). *Somatic experiencing: 10 best exercises & examples.* PositivePsychology.com. https://positivepsychology.com/somatic-experiencing/

Raypole, C. (2022, September 30). *Get over guilt with these steps.* Healthline. https://www.healthline.com/health/mental-health/how-to-stop-feeling-guilty

Raypole, C. (2023, March 17). *Pressure points for anxiety: 6 points to try for relief.* Healthline. https://www.healthline.com/health/pressure-points-for-anxiety

Rebecca. (2023). *Self abandonment: 10 ways to stop abandoning yourself.* Minimalism Made Simple. https://www.minimalismmadesimple.com/home/self-abandonment/

Reflecting on your belief system. (n.d.). Living Harbor. https://livingharbor.com/belief-system/

Rehab Blog. (n.d.). *Fort behavioral health.* https://www.fortbehavioral.com/addiction-recovery-blog/

Reina's story on intergenerational trauma & spirituality. (2023, January 13). Kids Help Phone. https://kidshelpphone.ca/get-info/reinas-story-on-intergenerational-trauma-spirituality/

Repression vs. suppression in psychology: Differences you didn't know. (2015, January 28). Psychologenie. https://psychologenie.com/repression-vs-suppression-in-psychology

Rewrite your story: change the meaning of your trauma. (2022, February 28). Serotinous Life. https://www.serotinouslife.com/blog/rewrite-your-story

Rice, A. (2022, January 5). *Trauma-informed mindfulness: A Guide.* Psych Central. https://psychcentral.com/health/trauma-informed-mindfulness

Robinson, B. (2020, June 22). *How movement and exercise can help ignite your creativity.* Thrive Global. https://community.thriveglobal.com/how-movement-and-exercise-can-help-ignite-your-creativity/

Roncero, A. (2021, October 22). *The unspoken truth about trauma: How it truly affects your life.* BetterUp. https://www.betterup.com/blog/trauma

Sacks, S. (2019, March 2). *Practicing trauma informed mindfulness meditation %. Safe passage.* https://safepass.org/2019/03/02/practicing-trauma-informed-mindfulness-meditation/

Salamon, M. (2023, July 7). *What is somatic therapy?* Harvard Health. https://www.health.harvard.edu/blog/what-is-somatic-therapy-202307072951

Salomon, S. H. (2022, August 7). *Trauma-informed fitness can help survivors heal through movement. Here's how.* https://www.livestrong.com/article/13769725-trauma-informed-fitness/

Schwartz, A. (2017, December 12). *Grounding | Dr. Arielle Schwartz.* Arielle Schwartz, PhD. https://drarielleschwartz.com/grounding-dr-arielle-schwartz/

Seattle Christian Counseling. (2020, August 21). *Engaging with God in the midst of trauma recovery.* Seattle Christian Counseling. https://seattlechristiancounseling.com/articles/engaging-with-god-in-the-midst-of-trauma-recovery

Self care and trauma. (2019, April 29). Promises FivePalms. https://sites.bu.edu/daniellerousseau/2019/04/29/self-care-and-trauma/

Self-care after trauma. (n.d.). RAINN. https://www.rainn.org/articles/self-care-after-trauma

Self-improvement. (n.d.). Verywell Mind. https://www.verywellmind.com/self-improvement-4157212

Sellers, R. (n.d.). *Refining trauma.* Rachel Sellers. https://www.rachelesellers.com/

7 hacks for better sleep. (n.d.). University of Colorado Boulder. https://www.colorado.edu/health/blog/sleep-hacks

7 trauma release exercises (TRE) to support your recovery after trauma. (2023, October 10). Ineffable Living. https://ineffableliving.com/7-trauma-release-exercises/

76 healing C-PTSD Quotes and affirmations + free printable flashcards. (n.d.). The Wellness Society | Self-Help, Therapy and Coaching Tools. https://thewellnesssociety.org/76-healing-cptsd-quotes-and-affirmations/

Shafir, H. (2022, July 29). *14 signs of repressed childhood trauma in adults.* Choosing Therapy. https://www.choosingtherapy.com/signs-of-repressed-childhood-trauma-in-adults/

Sharma, S. (2021, December 30). *Trauma denial: why it is important to address.* Calm Sage. https://www.calmsage.com/what-is-trauma-denial/

Shippert, P. (2019, May 31). *10 ways to boost trauma therapy: #10 Drumming in Community.* Peg Shippert, MA, LPC. https://www.pegshippert.com/blog/2019/5/31/10-ways-to-boost-trauma-therapy-10-drumming-in-community

Sholl, J. (2022, March 22). *7 tips on eating for trauma recovery.* Experience Life. https://experiencelife.lifetime.life/article/7-tips-on-eating-for-trauma-recovery/

Signs of emotional trauma in adults: recognizing and addressing the symptoms | All Points North. (2023, June 20). All Points North. https://apn.com/resources/signs-of-emotional-trauma-in-adults-recognizing-and-addressing-the-symptoms/

Signs of mental trauma. (n.d.). FHE Health. https://fherehab.com/trauma/signs-symptoms

Signs of repressed childhood trauma in adults. (2021, August 16). Integrative Life Center. https://integrativelifecenter.com/signs-of-repressed-childhood-trauma-in-adults/

Simbra, M. (2023, August 8). *Narrative exposure therapy (NET): What it is, cost, & how it works.* Choosing Therapy. https://www.choosingtherapy.com/narrative-exposure-therapy/

6 reasons why you should celebrate success. (2015, August 1). *Brilliant Living HQ.* https://www.brilliantlivinghq.com/6-reasons-why-you-should-celebrate-success/

Solutions to trauma: acupuncture for trauma. (2020, July 23). Trauma Thrivers. https://traumathrivers.com/solutions-to-trauma-acupuncture-for-trauma/

Spiritual treatment. (n.d.). Rehab Spot. https://www.rehabspot.com/treatment/spiritual/

Spring, C. (2021, September 7). *Why it's hard to heal from trauma | three challenges of trauma.* Carolyn Spring. https://www.carolynspring.com/blog/three-challenges-of-trauma-why-recovery-is-so-hard/

Spring, C. (n.d.). *Understanding trauma.* Carolyn Spring. https://www.carolynspring.com/trauma/

Stanton, R. (2021, December 13). *7 myths about trauma. Counseling in Boston* llc. https://counselinginboston.com/7-myths-about-trauma/

Stephanie M. Hutchins Quote: (n.d.). Quotefancy.com. https://quotefancy.com/quote/3766522/stephanie-m-hutchins-trauma-doesn-t-disappear-when-you-ignore-it

Suarez-Jimenez, B. (2022, December 7). *Researchers reveal how trauma changes the brain.* URMC Newsroom. https://www.urmc.rochester.edu/news/

publications/neuroscience/researchers-reveal-how-trauma-changes-the-brain

Sutton, J. (2019, January 3). *What is resilience, and why is it important to bounce back?* PositivePsychology.com. https://positivepsychology.com/what-is-resilience/#what-is-resilience

Swaim, E. (2022, May 28). *How narrative therapy could help heal complex trauma.* Healthline. https://www.healthline.com/health/mental-health/narrative-therapy-for-trauma

Sweeney, M. (2019, August 21). *Trauma and sleep: How to cope.* Start Sleeping. https://startsleeping.org/trauma-and-sleep/

Tedeschi, R. G. (2020, July 1). *Growth after trauma.* Harvard Business Review. https://hbr.org/2020/07/growth-after-trauma#:~:text=Post-traumatic%20growth%20often%20happens%20naturally%2C%20T-edeschi%20says%2C%20but

Teller, S. (2020, May 7). *Developing a growth mindset after trauma.* Sara E. Teller. https://sarateller.com/developing-a-growth-mindset-after-trauma/

10 somatic interventions explained. (n.d.). *Integrative Psychotherapy & Trauma Treatment.* https://integrativepsych.co/new-blog/somatic-therapy-explained-methods

Theresa. (2023, September 21). *Pendulation in trauma therapy.* Dis-Sos.com. https://www.dis-sos.com/pendulation-in-trauma-therapy/

Tigar, L. (2021, February 4). *How to be more patient with yourself.* Fast Company. https://www.fastcompany.com/90621058/how-to-be-more-patient-with-yourself

Todd, B. (2021, March). *How to identify your personal strengths.* 80,000 Hours. https://80000hours.org/articles/personal-strengths/

Top 4 steps to practice PTSD mindfulness exercises (safely). (2023, June 22). Ineffable Living. https://ineffableliving.com/use-mindfulness-safely-to-heal-from-trauma/#3-

Tosin. (2021, April 28). *10 obvious signs you need a self-care day ASAP.* The Insignificant Soul. https://thebeautyinbeinginsignificant.com/signs-need-self-care-day/

Trauma narratives (Guide). (2016, September 5). Therapist Aid. https://www.therapistaid.com/therapy-guide/trauma-narratives

Trauma symptoms. (n.d.). The Trauma Practice. https://traumapractice.co.uk/trauma-symptoms/

Trauma-informed mindfulness. (2023, March 1). *Calm Classroom.* https://blog.calmclassroom.com/trauma-informed-mindfulness

Trauma. (2023, October). American Psychological Association. https://www.apa.org/topics/trauma

Trauma: it's not what you think and why that matters. (2022, April 15). Psycom. https://www.psycom.net/trauma

Treatment essentials. (n.d.). U.S. Department of Veterans Affairs. https://www.ptsd.va.gov/professional/treat/txessentials/

Treatment. (2023, October 20). National Elf Service. https://www.nationalelfservice.net/treatment/

Treatments for PTSD. (n.d.). APA. https://www.apa.org/ptsd-guideline/treatments/

Treleaven, D. (2019, June 4). What's trauma-sensitive mindfulness? *Mindful Leader.* https://www.mindfulleader.org/blog/26483-what-s-trauma-sensitive-

Truitt, K. (2019, December 23). *Self-care after trauma.* Trauma Counseling Center of Los Angeles. https://traumacounseling.com/trauma-therapy-blog/self-care-after-trauma/

Tull, M. (2021, September 6). *What is cognitive processing therapy (CPT)?* Verywell Mind. https://www.verywellmind.com/cognitive-processing-therapy-2797281

Types of mental health problems. (n.d.). Mind. https://www.mind.org.uk/information-support/types-of-mental-health-problems/

Types of resilience. (n.d.). Community Industry Group. https://communityindustrygroup.org.au/lessons/types-of-resilience/

Types of trauma. (n.d.). The Trauma Practice. https://traumapractice.co.uk/types-of-trauma/

Vallejo, M. (2023, March 7). 25 best childhood trauma quotes. *Mental Health Center Kids.* https://mentalhealthcenterkids.com/blogs/articles/childhood-trauma-quotes

Van Derbur, M. (n.d.). *Marilyn Van Derbur quotes.* Goodreads. https://www.goodreads.com/quotes/429448-all-emotions-even-those-that-are-suppressed-and-unexpressed-have

Vaughn, S. (n.d.). *DBT interpersonal effectiveness skills: Managing relationships and strategies for communication.* Psychotherapy Academy. https://psychotherapyacademy.org/section/interpersonal-effectiveness-module/

Waehner, P. (2021, October 5). *Motivation for exercise.* Verywell Fit. https://www.verywellfit.com/fitness-motivation-4157145

Waichler, I. (2022, June 9). *Post traumatic growth: finding meaning after trauma.* Choosing Therapy. https://www.choosingtherapy.com/post-traumatic-growth/

Wang, Z., Jiang, B., Wang, X., Li, Z., Wang, D., Xue, H., & Wang, D. (2023). Relationship between physical activity and individual mental health after traumatic events: a systematic review. *A Systematic Review, 14(2).* https://doi.org/10.1080/20008066.2023.2205667

WebMD Editorial Contributors. (2021, April 12). *What is narrative therapy?* WebMD. https://www.webmd.com/mental-health/what-is-narrative-therapy

Week 5—grab hold of life. (n.d.). Bear Psychology Trauma Practice Traumatology Institute. https://whatisptsd.com/week-5-2/

What is choosing therapy? (n.d.). Choosing Therapy. https://www.choosingtherapy.com/

What is Neuro Somatic therapy? (n.d.). All Things Autoimmunity. https://allthingsautoimmunity.com/what-is-neuro-somatic-therapy/

What is somatic experiencing? (n.d.). Somatic Experiencing International. https://traumahealing.org/se-101/

What is somatic psychotherapy. (n.d.). Genesis Recovery San Diego. https://www.genesisrecovery.com/somatic-psychotherapy/

What we think about. (2020, March 19). Align Grand Cayman. https://www.align.ky/what-we-think-about

White, T. (2022, May 13). *Repressed trauma: Signs, symptoms, and what to do.* Psych Central. https://psychcentral.com/ptsd/repressed-trauma#vs-

Wipfli, S. (2022, June 21). *Top misconceptions about trauma busted.* Stanley E. Wipfli, LCSW, MAC Psychotherapist. https://stanleywipfli.com/top-misconceptions-about-trauma-busted/

Wooll, M. (2021, July 26). *A growth mindset is a must-have — these 13 tips Will grow yours.* Betterup. https://www.betterup.com/blog/growth-mindset

Yin, X., Li, W., Liang, T., Lu, B., Yue, H., Li, S., Zhong, V. W., Zhang, W., Li, X., Zhou, S., Mi, Y., Wu, H., & Xu, S. (2022). Effect of electroacupuncture on insomnia in patients with depression. *JAMA Network Open, 5(7)*, e2220563. https://doi.org/10.1001/jamanetworkopen.2022.20563

Zwarensteyn, J. (2021, October 29). *48 sleep hacks - how to get the best sleep of your life, every night!* Sleep Advisor. https://www.sleepadvisor.org/48-sleep-hacks/References